Mindfulness and Meditation for Adolescents

Betsy L. Wisner

Mindfulness and Meditation for Adolescents

Practices and Programs

Betsy L. Wisner
Our Lady of the Lake University
San Antonio, Texas, USA

ISBN 978-1-349-95206-9 ISBN 978-1-349-95207-6 (eBook)
DOI 10.1057/978-1-349-95207-6

Library of Congress Control Number: 2017939141

Printed on acid-free paper

This Palgrave Macmillan imprint is published by Springer Nature
The registered company is Nature America Inc.
The registered company address is: 1 New York Plaza, New York, NY 10004, U.S.A.

This book is dedicated to my family, friends, and to the many adolescents who have touched my life. Thank you.

Acknowledgments

I have had the privilege of working with adolescents and their families in counseling, correctional, and school settings. I served in various capacities in these settings, including counselor, family therapist, and school social worker. At the same time that I worked in the helping professions, I also taught developmental psychology courses, including adolescent psychology.

These experiences provided a solid foundation for my research exploring the benefits of school-based mindfulness meditation programming for adolescents. However, it was my experience as a student in Dr. David Springer's class on Direct Social Work Practice at The University of Texas at Austin that lead to my research with adolescents. It was Dr. Springer's expertise in working with adolescents and his openness to mindfulness practices that stimulated my own idea to complete a dissertation on mindfulness with adolescents. Dr. Springer has remained a mentor, and I am grateful for his support over the years. He has assisted me with each milestone of my academic career including encouragement while writing this book.

I was in the right place at the right time. When I conducted my dissertation research, there were only a handful of publications on mindfulness and adolescents. Now, even though adolescents continue to be under-served in many settings, there are many studies on this topic.

In my current role as faculty member teaching social work courses for graduate students, I recognize the importance of drawing on my knowledge and expertise to contribute to the profession. I can think of no better way to do that than to promote the use of mindfulness and meditation practices for youth. Thus, the purpose of this book is to provide graduate students, educators, clinicians, and researchers interested in mindfulness and meditation practices and programs for youth with an overview and synthesis of the literature and research about these programs. I hope this book provides helpful information to those interested in mindfulness and meditation programming for youth.

My commissioning editor at Palgrave Macmillan, Rachel Krause, deserves recognition for her professionalism and support from our initial communication through the completion of this book. She answered my many questions and supported my development as a first-time book author. I also am thankful to Kyra Saniewski, Editorial Assistant at Palgrave Macmillan, for her guidance during the writing process.

My niece, Kirsten Hollenbeck, helped to edit the early chapter drafts and used her expertise with adolescents to help me create the case examples used in this book. I appreciate her help.

I'd like to thank my mother, Patricia Dafoe, my sister, Deborah Hollenbeck, and my brothers, Jay Wisner, Daniel Wisner, and Andrew Wisner for their friendship and support. They have supported all my dreams.

I have had the unique opportunity to co-facilitate a mindfulness program, conduct research, and collaborate on publications with my partner and husband, James Starzec. I appreciate his wise counsel and helpful support through the many adventures we have experienced together.

Contents

List of Figures

List of Tables

CHAPTER 1

An Introduction to Mindfulness and Meditation Practices and Programs for Adolescents

Introduction

Adolescence, with its opportunities and risks, is one of the most exciting and challenging phases of life. The range of experiences for adolescents is diverse – a 15-year-old girl may be spending 4 hours a day after school preparing for athletic competitions, another 15-year-old girl heads to a shelter after school as her home has been destroyed by shelling; a third 15-year-old girl pulls out her cell phone as soon as she boards her school bus and connects with her friends through Snapchat and Facebook. In these situations, adults are positioned to provide support and guidance for these youths. This book incorporates the actual voices of adolescents to illustrate the benefits that mindfulness and meditation practices offer for contemporary adolescents. Whether adolescents require help in stressful circumstances or need support for positive developmental experiences, mindfulness and meditation practices may be beneficial for them.

Adolescents work through these developmental tasks and opportunities in the contexts of home, neighborhoods, schools, and spiritual and religious groups and through caring relationships with family members, peers, friends, and supportive adults. Adolescents who need assistance meeting developmental challenges may be offered any number of broad options from within biological, psychological, social, and cultural contexts to help them successfully navigate adolescence. General interventions and activities within these contexts have traditionally included psychopharmacology regimens, counseling, peer mentoring programs, sports programs, stress management, and educational

B.L. Wisner, *Mindfulness and Meditation for Adolescents*,
DOI 10.1057/978-1-349-95207-6_1

programs. It is imperative that these interventions meet the unique developmental needs and optimize the strengths of particular adolescents. In addition, intervention options are enhanced by a broader compendium of approaches that incorporate neurobiology and promote positive youth development (Norton, 2011). Mindfulness and meditation practices are among these innovative approaches that promote self-regulation, stress reduction, and wellness for adolescents. These practices have demonstrated a wide range of positive biological, psychological, cognitive, and social effects with few contraindications (Black, 2015; Wisner & Starzec, 2011).

Mindfulness and meditation practices may be used as complementary interventions in conjunction with traditional approaches and through independent programs. These practices and programs for adolescents are offered in diverse settings, including counseling, behavioral health, medical, educational, and community settings. Thus, it is important to offer contemporary mindfulness and meditation practices for adolescents with an understanding of the broader context of adolescent development. This book offers an overview and synthesis of the evidence-base for the efficacy of these diverse programs. Examples of successful programs along with suggestions for improving the developmentally appropriate design and delivery of these programs for adolescents are offered. In addition, it highlights models that address the unique needs of the adolescents in clinical, educational, residential, and community settings. This literature is presented in a context consistent with evidence-based practice and current theoretical foundations of meditation, mindfulness, and adolescence. This chapter provides the foundation for these goals by providing the historical contexts of meditation, mindfulness, and adolescence, offering clear definitions of these concepts, and a thorough introduction to relevant literature.

Historical Contexts and Definition of Meditation and Mindfulness

Forms of meditation have historically been used as contemplative religious and spiritual practices. Examples of these practices and paths include centering prayer in Christianity (Keating, 1988), Internal Alchemy in Daoism (Roth, 2015), forms of Yoga in Hinduism (Bryant, 2015), Sufism in Islam (Esposito, Fasching, Lewis, & Bowlby, 2002), Zazen in Zen Buddhism (Thomson, 2000), Kabbalah in Judaism (Magid, 2015), and South Asian Buddhist Vipassana meditation (Komjathy, 2015). In particular, religious and philosophical systems such as Buddhism, Taoism, and Confucianism maintain a focus on awareness, centering, mindfulness, and meditation (Hwang, 2011). Moreover, meditative practices may serve as integral aspects of spiritual practices for those from Indigenousness communities (Hart, 2010). Secular mindfulness and meditation practices, although not religious in nature, often include elements extracted from religious forms of practice. Thus, in secularized practices, religious components are typically minimized or eliminated in order to formulate the secular practice.

Given the diverse religious, spiritual, and secular forms of meditation, providing a coherent definition of meditation is challenging. This concern reduces the clarity of discussions of meditation and may limit effectiveness of research conducted on meditation (Lutz, Slagter, Dunne, & Davidson, 2008). The secular literature on meditation often characterizes meditation with an emphasis on processes of concentration and mindfulness. Concentrative methods typically involve focusing attention on an object. Alternatively, mindfulness, as the foundation for various meditation practices, involves awareness. For example, Lutz et al. (2008) suggested that various methods of meditation may be viewed as either focused attention (FA) or open monitoring (OM). These two categories are based on the process of meditation and the neurological implications of the meditation. Focused attention involves maintaining attention on an object with awareness of distractions and a consequent return to attention on the object. Open monitoring involves observation and awareness of experience without reacting to the content of experience. More recently, however, it has been recognized that categorizing meditation into concentration and mindfulness practices is a simplistic approach since many types of meditation include a combination of these methods (Sedlmeier et al., 2012).

Nash and Newberg (2013) addressed this concern by differentiating between the method of meditation (i.e., the instructions, procedures, and techniques used to regulate attention and emotion) and the state of meditation (the enhanced mental state brought about by the meditation method). This approach encompasses secular, religious, and spiritual meditation methods. Nash and Newberg (2013) suggest that meditation methods may be classified into three domains: cognitive-directed methods (e.g., Samatha, Vipassana, Kirtan Kriya, Tai Chi Chuan, mindfulness), affective-directed methods (e.g., compassion and loving-kindness techniques), and null-directed methods (e.g., TM). Cognitive-directed methods emphasize practices such as one-pointedness and mindfulness. Affective-directed methods emphasize enhancing emotional states, while null-directed methods involve an "enhanced empty state that is devoid of phenomenological content" (p. 6). These meditation methods may be used to bring about unique benefits of enhanced cognitive and emotional states, stress reduction, wellness, and attainment of wisdom and enlightenment (Nash & Newberg, 2013).

Mindfulness, in a secular context, may be defined as "the awareness that emerges through paying attention on purpose, in the present moment, and nonjudgmentally to the unfolding of experience moment by moment" (Kabat-Zinn, 2003, p. 147). Mindfulness is also viewed as attending to present-moment experience with acceptance and without elaborating on thoughts or feelings (Bishop et al., 2004; Teasdale, Segal, & Williams, 1995). Mindfulness forms the foundation for the secularized intervention of mindfulness-based stress reduction (MBSR). This group-based intervention integrates mindfulness and Hatha yoga practices for use in secular wellness and stress management programs and settings (Kabat-Zinn, 1990). In a discussion of the religious roots of mindfulness practices, Komjathy (2015) describes MBSR as a "medicalized version of South Asian Buddhist Vipassana meditation" (p. 604). Kabat-Zinn (2011) provides a comprehensive discussion of the Buddhist influences on the development of MBSR but suggests that mindfulness may be viewed as universal in nature, and in that sense, the definition is not restricted to a particular spiritual or religious context (Kabat-Zinn, 2003).

Mindfulness-based stress reduction, and a number of other secularized practices, were developed with the purpose of alleviating symptoms and restoring health. These practices emerged from the field of mind-body medicine (Komjathy, 2015), and also include the Relaxation Response (Benson, 1975; Benson & Proctor, 2010) and the Center for Mind-Body Medicine's (CMBM) model of community-based intervention that incorporates meditative practices (Gordon, 1996). Transcendental Meditation (TM), originally developed for expanding consciousness, is also recognized for its ability to reduce stress and to improve general health and well-being (Bloomfield, Cain, Jaffe, & Kory, 1975; Rosenthal, 2012).

In this book, the focus is on secular meditation practices for adolescents as presented in the scholarly literature addressing medical, mental health, and wellness benefits. All of these practices and programs were developed for use with adults and have now been adapted for use with adolescents. However, the literature in this area is still in its infancy and therefore it is crucial to provide solid grounding in the historical and theoretical foundations when offering these programs to adolescents. Providing a clear definition of adolescence provides a foundation from which to fully address the literature about mindfulness and meditation programming and research provided in subsequent chapters.

Definition and Historical Contexts of Adolescence

Interestingly, adolescence is sometimes defined by what it is not. Adolescence is not childhood, it is not adulthood; adolescence is a bridge between childhood and adulthood. G. Stanley Hall (1904) considered adolescence to be the time period from 14–24 years of age. However, over time views of adolescence have changed and adolescence is now typically considered to span the range of 10–18 or 19 years of age (Arnett, 2000; World Health Organization, 2016).

Hall (1904) had suggested that adolescence commenced at age 14, while we now consider adolescence to begin as early as 10 years of age. This, in part, is driven by trends toward earlier puberty as a result of a complex interaction of genetic, health, nutrition, and environmental factors (Parent, Teilmann, Juul, Skakkebaek, Toppari, & Bourguignon, 2003). Ideas also are offered to explain the changes to the upper age limit of adolescence. For example, three major social movements contributed to the current understanding of adolescence as ending at 18 or 19 years of age (Bakan, 1971). These contributing factors, dating to the early to mid-1900s, involved legislation of compulsory education, child labor, and treatment of young people in the justice system. In order to offer specific legislation to protect children and adolescents, there had to be a legal definition of adulthood. Thus, adolescence was deemed to end at the age adulthood began (typically, 18 years of age).

Another contemporary factor contributing to the view that adolescence ends at 18 or 19 years of age is related to the marked differences in developmental tasks between those in their late teens and those in their early twenties (Arnett, 2000; Erikson, 1968). Thus, Arnett suggests that adolescents be differentiated from those in their early twenties; he considers the developmental stage from 18–25 years of age to be a unique and transitional stage labeled emerging adulthood.

In addition, adolescence was once considered a time of "storm and stress" (Hall, 1904). While we no longer view adolescence in this manner, it is still considered one of the most stressful times of life (Arnett, 1999; Spear, 2000).

Three of the primary factors related to this stress involve conflict with parents, engaging in high-risk behaviors, and experiencing difficulties related to emotions (Arnett, 1999). However, while many adolescents experience serious challenges during the navigation of adolescence, many do not experience major or lasting concerns (Arnett, 1999; Spear, 2000). In fact, for transitions related to emotional arousal factors, adolescents show a wide range of individual differences in the length and intensity of these transitions. Moreover, stress levels may be modulated by development of emotional regulation skills that can positively influence how life transitions are experienced (Hollenstein & Lougheed, 2013).

Given these factors related to adolescent development, it is crucial that adolescents have access to methods to manage stress, improve emotional regulation skills, and promote strengths that assist them in navigating these life transitions. Research on contemporary practices and programs derived primarily from the field of mind-body medicine show that mindfulness and meditation programs help adolescents in all of these areas. These programs have been shown to help adolescents reduce stress (Barnes, Bauza, & Treiber, 2003; Rawlett, & Scrandis, 2015), develop self-regulation skills (Barnes, Davis, Murzynowski, & Treiber, 2004; Rosaen & Benn, 2006), and enhance behavioral and emotional strengths (Grabbe, Nguy, & Higgins, 2012; Niemiec, Rashid, & Spinella, 2012; Wisner & Norton, 2013).

A number of key individuals and organizations have contributed to the contemporary use of mindfulness and meditation practices and programs for adults, and have provided the primary platforms for designing mindfulness and meditation programs for adolescents. Thus, these influences are explored to provide an understanding of the contexts in which programs for adolescents developed.

Contemporary Pioneers of Mindfulness and Meditation Programs

Integration of mindfulness practices and programs in secular settings has been influenced by the pioneering work of Jon Kabat-Zinn and the University of Massachusetts Center for Mindfulness, and through Congressman Tim Ryan's efforts to bring mindfulness into the mainstream in the United States. Mantra-based meditation practices, such as TM and the Relaxation Response, also have provided the impetus for meditation programs. In addition, the CMBM has incorporated meditative practices in their work with those from traumatized communities. An introduction to these contemporary influences is provided here and the related literature on these programs for adolescents is explored in more detail in subsequent chapters.

Jon Kabat-Zinn and Popularization of Mindfulness

Jon Kabat-Zinn, as the founding director of the Mindfulness and Stress Reduction Clinic (MSRC) at the University of Massachusetts Medical Center, has been instrumental in integrating secular mindfulness and Hatha yoga practices into wellness and stress management programs and settings. The MSRC's Stress Reduction and Relaxation Program, with its inception in 1979, stimulated a burgeoning use of mindfulness practices in the United States and other countries. Kabat-Zinn (1990) introduced the promise of mindfulness (for stress management and pain reduction) to the general public in his book, *Full Catastrophe Living: Using the Wisdom of Your Body and Mind to Face Stress, Pain and Illness.* The MSRC's manualized program, MBSR, evolved over the years and helps patients reduce physical and psychological symptoms (Kabat-Zinn, 1990). As such, it is now used as a complementary intervention to treat a wide range of medical and emotional conditions (Kabat-Zinn, 2011).

Mindfulness practices, as articulated by Kabat-Zinn and the MSRC, have provided the impetus for integration of mindfulness programs for adults in medical, educational, counseling, and behavioral health settings (Cullen, 2011). Cullen addresses the rapid growth and broad scope of Mindfulness-Based Interventions (MBIs) since publication of Segal, Williams, and Teasdale's (2002) work on mindfulness-based cognitive therapy for depression. She illustrates the global nature of this expansion and points out that,

> There is now a graduate program in MBCT at Oxford University and the British National Health Service pays for the cost of the program. Another prominent mindfulness center in the United Kingdom is the Centre for Mindfulness Research and Practice at Bangor University. Numerous other MBIs have been spawned from MBSR including: Mindfulness-Based Childbirth and Parenting, SMART in Education/Mindfulness-Based Emotional Balance, Cool Minds™ (for adolescents), A Still Quiet Place (children of all ages), Mindfulness-Based Eating, Mindfulness-Based Relapse Prevention, Mindfulness-Based Elder Care, Mindfulness-Based Mental Fitness Training, Mindfulness-Based Art Therapy for Cancer

> Patients, Mindful Leadership™, Mindful Schools, Mindfulness without Borders, Trauma Sensitive MBSR for women with PTSD, along with many other programs designed for specific age groups from pre-school through higher education. Norway, Sweden, Holland, France, Ireland, Germany, South Africa, Switzerland, and Italy are among many countries that have institutes and national associations of mindfulness teachers and trainings. (Cullen, 2011, p. 3–4)

Undoubtedly, additional programs will continue to emerge, and many of the practices that are used with adolescents are loosely based on MBSR for adults (Schoeberlein & Koffler, 2005). In subsequent chapters, an overview of studies conducted with mindfulness programs adapted for adolescents is provided along with examples of mindfulness programs in educational, counseling, behavioral health, medical, residential, and community settings.

Congressman Tim Ryan and the Mindfulness Revolution

Tim Ryan, U.S. Representative from Ohio's 13th Congressional District, is on a mission to introduce mindfulness to a wide audience. Following a personal experience with mindfulness training through one of the MSRCs five-day mindfulness retreats, he began to share his message of the power of mindfulness practices and promote what he calls the mindfulness revolution. He does so through frequent guest appearances at conferences, meetings, and events. In addition, his book, *A Mindful Nation: How a Simple Practice Can Help Us Reduce Stress, Improve Performance, and Recapture the American Spirit*, provides a clear overview of the benefits of mindfulness with a particular emphasis on benefits for students, medical patients, and those in the military (Ryan, 2012).

Ryan also initiated regular sessions encouraging quiet reflection for both House Members and Staffers (Bendery, 2013). In addition, he promotes the role of mindfulness practices and programs for children and adolescents through introduction of legislation to support educational programming for social and emotional learning in schools. One example is the Academic, Social, and Emotional Learning Act of 2015–HR 850 (http://timryan.house.gov/legislative-work). He also has secured funding for mindfulness programs for schools in his congressional district (Cogen, 2015).

While mindfulness practices and programs for adolescents have proliferated, mantra-based practices and programs have shown promise as well. Two of these practices are now discussed: Transcendental Meditation (TM) and the Benson-Henry Protocol to elicit the Relaxation Response.

Maharishi Mahesh Yogi and Transcendental Meditation

Transcendental Meditation was developed in the 1950s, by Maharishi Mahesh Yogi, as a means to access transcendent states of consciousness (Bloomfield, Cain, Jaffe, & Kory, 1975). The book, *TM: Discovering Inner Energy and Overcoming Stress* introduced the benefits of TM to the general public (Bloomfield et al., 1975). While developed from a spiritual or religious practice, TM often is used in secular settings and contexts for stress management and as a complementary intervention to manage health conditions such as hypertension. Transcendental Meditation is a technique that uses a mantra (i.e., a sound with no meaning) and does not involve concentration or control of the mind. The technique, leading to an alert but restful state, is taught to individuals through a standardized format over the course of four consecutive days by certified meditation teachers. Tuition includes this initial training plus follow-up sessions (Rosenthal, 2012).

While now described as a secular practice (e.g., www.tm.org), some contend that TM maintains aspects of religious practice. Komjathy (2015) described the comparative secularization of TM when he stated that TM is a, "relatively secularized form of meditation" (p. 616). He pointed out that, "At the very least, it is a reconceptualized and decontextualized form of Hindu religious practice" (p. 616). To illustrate this point, Komjathy (2015) provides an example of this comparative secularization in TM in which the student of TM is assigned a personal and secret mantra comprised of Sanskrit sounds by a certified meditation teacher sanctioned by the Maharishi Foundation.

The TM method, originally designed for adults, is now offered to children and adolescents. For example, the David Lynch Foundation operates a grant program to provide TM instruction to at-risk youth in school-based settings (www.davidlynchfoundation.org). An overview of studies of TM programs for adolescents is offered in Chapter 3, while examples of school-based TM programs are presented in Chapter 4.

Herbert Benson and the Relaxation Response

Herbert Benson, a cardiologist, founded the Benson-Henry Institute for Mind Body Medicine (formally the Mind Body Medical Institute) at Massachusetts General Hospital (www.massgeneral.org). Benson, now the Director Emeritus of the Benson-Henry Institute (BHI) and Mind Body Medicine Professor of Medicine at the Harvard Medical School, initiated research on the benefits of TM in the 1960s. Benson speculated that the benefits of methods such as TM could be achieved through secular practices and he eventually developed a protocol for a secular mantra-based meditation method for stress management (the Relaxation Response). This method was popularized through his first book, *The Relaxation Response* (Benson, 1975, 2000) and through many subsequent books and publications (see www.bensonhenryinstitute.org/about/dr-herbert-benson for a comprehensive list of these sources).

This meditation method incorporates the use of a secular mantra (typically a word or phrase) and induces the Relaxation Response (RR), a state that is characterized as the opposite of the flight-or-fight stress response. This is a physiological state of alert calmness marked by muscle relaxation and decreased blood pressure, heart rate, and respiration (Benson & Proctor, 2010). With the emphasis on a secular mantra and the health benefits of the practice, this method is considered to be a therapeutic, "medicalized," and secularized form of meditation (Komjathy, 2015, p. 604).

Although the protocol remains secular in nature, since the publication of Benson's initial book in 1975, the importance of factors related to faith, spirituality, and belief are addressed in subsequent books (Benson, 2000; Benson, 2009; Benson & Proctor, 2010). Benson (2000) also clarified that the necessary components for eliciting the RR are a mental device and a passive attitude, and that the RR may be elicited by mantra meditation or other activities such as yoga, qigong, or swimming. Methods to elicit the RR have been adapted for use with adolescents and incorporated into schools through the Resilient Schools program (http://www.bensonhenryinstitute.org/services/resilient-schools). Chapter 3 addresses literature, examining the effectiveness of the Relaxation Response with adolescent populations, while Chapter 4 includes examples of school-based programs for adolescents.

James Gordon and the Center for Mind-Body Medicine

James S. Gordon, a psychiatrist, is the Founder and Executive Director of the Center for Mind-Body Medicine and a Clinical Professor in the Departments of Psychiatry and Family Medicine at Georgetown Medical School. Gordon's (1996) book, *Manifesto for a New Medicine: Your Guide to Healing Partnerships and the Wise Use of Alternative Therapies* describes his approach to healing. Gordon developed a mind-body program that incorporates practices such as meditation and qigong. This approach features a group treatment modality to help those experiencing emotional stress and psychological trauma. Gordon's model has been used to promote healing in communities devastated by war, oppression, and natural catastrophes (http://cmbm.org). More information about the evidence base for this approach with adolescents is offered in Chapter 3, and examples of how adolescents and their communities have been helped through this work are provided in Chapter 4 (school-based programs) and Chapter 6 (community-based programs).

Mindfulness and Meditation Literature and Research Base: An Introduction

This section aims to provide an overview of the trends in research examining the effectiveness of mindfulness and meditation with an emphasis on approaches for adolescents. In order to provide cogent information about the current state of the evidence about mindfulness and meditation programs, it is helpful to address the progression of the literature and resources on this topic. For example, there are now a number of resources for adolescents and scholarly books for those who work with this population. A list of books and websites that provide resources for adolescents, professionals working with adolescents, and parents of adolescents may be found at the end of this chapter. Some of these resources are highlighted in this section, along with discussion of peer-reviewed journal articles on this topic.

Books for Adolescents and Scholarly Books for Parents and Professionals

While the seminal books by mind-body medicine pioneers (Benson, 1975, 2000; Bloomfield et al., 1975; Gordon, 1996; Kabat-Zinn, 1990; Ryan, 2012) presented information about the healing potential of secular mindfulness and meditation, these books typically address practices with adults and do not emphasize the specific developmental challenges of adolescence. However, there are books oriented toward mindfulness practices and programs for adolescents and their parents and for professionals working with adolescents. Books targeted toward those offering mindfulness practices and programs for adolescents include Rechtschaffen's (2014), *The Way of Mindful Education: Cultivating Well-being in Teachers and Students,* Saltzman's (2014), *A Still Quiet Place: A Mindfulness Program for Teaching Children and Adolescents to Ease Stress and Difficult Emotions,* and Broderick's (2013), *Learning to Breathe: A Mindfulness Curriculum for Adolescents to Cultivate Emotion Regulation, Attention, and Performance.* In addition, Greco and Hayes (2008) offer a guide for behavioral health practitioners in their book, *Acceptance and Mindfulness Treatments for Children and Adolescents: A Practitioner's Guide.*

Two books oriented toward teen readers include Saltzman's (2016), *A Still Quiet Place for Teens: A Mindfulness Workbook to Ease Stress and Difficult Emotions* and Biegel's (2010) book, *The Stress Reduction Workbook for Teens: Mindfulness Skills to Help You Deal with Stress.* In addition, Greenland (2010) authored a book specifically for parents, *The Mindful Child: How to Help Your Kid Manage Stress and Become Happier, Kinder, and More Compassionate.*

These books for adolescents and those who work with and care for adolescents are often grounded in a sound developmental perspective; however, they do not address the broader spectrum of meditative strategies that show promise for alleviating stress, enhancing self-regulation, and promoting strengths for adolescents. This book aims to address this concern by providing a broader overview of these programs and practices.

Peer-Reviewed Literature

There were few scholarly articles or research studies published on secular mindfulness and meditation prior to 1990s. Vago (2016) illustrates the expansion of the research on meditative practices and programs in a graph showing the number of peer-reviewed publications of studies in these areas from the 1990s through 2014 (Figure 1.1: https://contemplativemind.wordpress.com/peer-reviewed-research-mindfulness-meditation-contemplative-practice/).

This graph shows the general increase of literature in this area and illustrates the significant increase in the number of published research studies after 2006. Studies on meditation and yoga show indications of

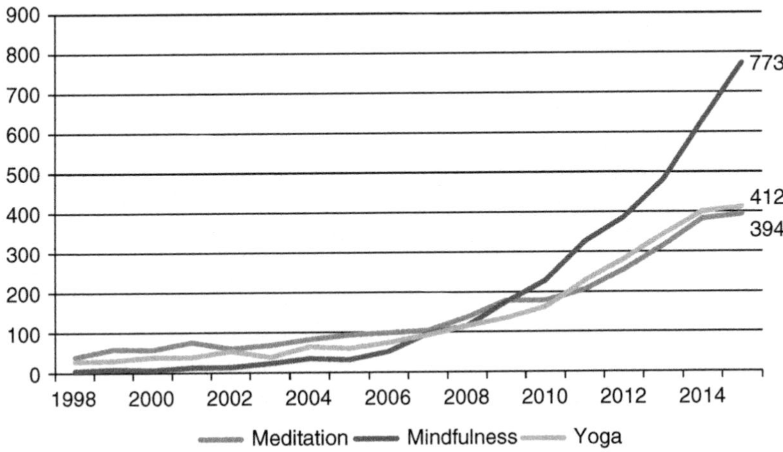

Fig. 1.1 Peer-reviewed research on mindfulness and meditation

leveling off in recent years while the growth of mindfulness studies continues the upward trajectory.

Not surprisingly, much of this published literature has addressed mindfulness for adults. Black (2015) reports that, of the 2,600 scholarly publications on mindfulness found through literature searches, less than 5% address work with children and adolescents. This is an obvious concern as these practices and programs have great potential for helping children and adolescents.

Research with Adults

Reviews and meta-analytic studies on meditation and mindfulness, primarily for adults, suggest that there are significant benefits to these programs. For example, in a review specific to mindfulness literature, Baer (2003) concluded that MBIs for clinical populations have the potential to reduce stress and to provide a means to cope with depression, anxiety, pain, eating disorders, personality disorders, and substance abuse. Eberth and Sedlmeier (2012) conducted a meta-analysis of studies of MBSR for non-clinical adult participants. They concluded that the main effect of

MBSR was on factors related to psychological well-being (e.g., reduction of stress, anxiety, and negative emotions). Khoury et al. (2013) reported that mindfulness-based therapy programs for clinical populations of adults brought about positive changes in relationships and decreases in depression, stress, and anxiety. In another meta-analytic study of mindfulness meditation programs for adults with mental health and medical conditions, meditation programs were found to bring about small to moderate reductions in anxiety, depression, and pain (Goyal et al., 2014).

In a comprehensive review of meditation programs (including mindfulness programs), Ospina et al. (2007) reviewed hundreds of studies that used meditation to address health-related concerns. They conducted meta-analyses on selected topics and concluded that most studies to date were of poor quality. However, they did suggest that meditation practices were helpful for reducing stress and hypertension. Similarly, in a meta-analysis of research studies with non-clinical adult participants, Sedlmeier et al. (2012) found that meditation interventions (including mindfulness, TM, and the RR) helped to improve relationships and reduce negative emotions and problematic cognitions. They also confirmed that meditation is not simply a relaxation technique; meditation yielded more pronounced effects than did relaxation alone, especially for reducing negative emotions and anxiety (Sedlmeier et al., 2012).

Research with Adolescents

Early literature reviews (e.g., Black, Milam, & Sussman, 2009; Burke, 2010; Wisner, Jones, & Gwin, 2010) found a small number of scholarly studies reporting on the use of mindfulness and meditation with adolescents. The majority of these early studies explored the impact of mindfulness practices and programs for adolescents (Barnes, Davis et al., 2004; Beauchemin, Hutchins, & Patterson, 2008; Biegel, Brown, Shapiro, & Schubert, 2009; Bogels, Hoogstad, van Dun, De Shutter, & Restifo, 2008; Bootzin & Stevens, 2005; Singh et al., 2007; Singh et al., 2008; Wall 2005; Wisner, 2008; Zylowska et al., 2008). Other studies explored the effects of TM programs (Barnes et al., 2003, Barnes, Treiber, & Davis, 2001; Barnes, Treiber, & Johnson, 2004; Rosaen & Benn, 2006; So & Orme-Johnson, 2001), and the Relaxation Response (Benson et al., 1994; Benson et al., 2000) with adolescent populations. The Center for Mind-Body Medicine's group program adapted for adolescents was also the focus of a study (Gordon, Staples, Blyta, & Bytyqi, 2004). In these early studies, we can see the trend in the preponderance of mindfulness studies (n=10), when compared with TM (n=5), the Relaxation Response (n=1), and the Center for Mind-Body Medicine's model (n=1). These studies found a wide range of bio-psycho-social-cultural benefits for adolescents and the results are explored in more detail in subsequent chapters.

The literature has expanded substantially since these early efforts and more comprehensive literature reviews and empirical studies assessing the efficacy of programs for adolescents are emerging. For example, Black (2015) reviewed studies of mindfulness training with both clinical and non-clinical samples of children and adolescents and reported a wide range of benefits of mindfulness programs. These benefits included improvements in prosocial skills, self-regulation, and attention, and reductions in anxiety, depression, perceived stress, blood pressure, and heart rate. The self-regulation benefits of mindfulness practices are particularly important for adolescents, and an example of this is provided by the following "Adolescent Voices" quote.

Adolescent Voices

"I'm more calm. I think before I do my actions because I don't want to flip out. I meditate when I get mad and I don't want to show it or anything."

Adolescent Mindfulness Skills Practitioner
(Wisner & Starzec, 2016, p. 252)

In addition, a meta-analytic study of mindfulness interventions with clinical and non-clinical samples of children and adolescents showed that mindfulness interventions for youth were helpful (Zoogman, Goldberg, Hoyt, & Miller, 2015). The authors concluded that mindfulness interventions increased mindfulness and attention and may be particularly beneficial for reducing anxiety and depression in clinical populations. Another meta-analytic study addressed school-based mindfulness programs for children and adolescents (Zenner, Herrnleben-Kurz, & Walach, 2014). Findings indicated that MBIs have the potential to improve cognitive performance, enhance resiliency, and reduce stress. Given the high levels of stress experienced by many adolescents, the potential for stress management benefits of meditation is important. The stress management benefits for adolescents are illustrated by the following "Adolescent Voices" quote.

Adolescent Voices

When I meditated, it felt like all my stress dropped to the floor and was replaced by relaxation.

Adolescent Mindfulness Meditation Practitioner
(Wisner, 2014, p. 633)

In addition to these meta-analyses, Felver, Celis-de Hoyos, Tezanos, & Singh (2016) conducted a systematic review of 28 studies of MBIs for youth in school settings. They concluded that MBIs in school settings have great potential for helping youth. The benefits to children and adolescents, as demonstrated by the studies they reviewed, included decreased behavioral problems, anxiety, depression, affective disturbances, executive functioning problems, and suicidal ideation. Also noted were improved positive affect, optimism, coping, emotion regulation, social-emotional competence, social skills, classroom engagement, and classroom behavior. Improvements in physiological functioning and increased mindfulness also were reported.

Summary

Adolescence, with both growth opportunities and personal risks, is best understood within a framework of historical and developmental factors. This framework provides the foundation for understanding the potential that a growing number of innovative mindfulness and meditation practices offer for adolescents. Incorporating empirical findings about these practices and programs while viewing them through the lens of historical and developmental factors provides a foundation for planning and delivering developmentally appropriate programs for youth. This approach also fosters program development that promotes benefits for adolescents, including increased self-regulation, stress reduction, wellness, and personal strengths.

Building on the foundation established in this chapter, Chapter 2 includes a targeted discussion of the theoretical foundations of adolescent development helpful for developing successful and developmentally appropriate mindfulness and meditation programs for adolescent populations. Chapter 3 presents a comprehensive review of the literature demonstrating the effectiveness of mindfulness and meditation practices and programs for adolescents. Examples of mindfulness and meditation programs in educational settings are presented in Chapter 4, while information about mindfulness programs in counseling, behavioral health, and medical settings is offered in Chapter 5. Chapter 6 provides information on mindfulness and meditation practices and programs in home, community-based, and specialized settings.

Resources

	Books
Benson (1975, 2000)	*The Relaxation Response*
Biegel (2010)	*The Stress Reduction Workbook for Teens: Mindfulness Skills to Help You Deal with Stress*
Bloomfield, Cain, Jaffe, and Kory (1975)	*TM: Discovering Inner Energy and Overcoming Stress*
Broderick (2013)	*Learning to Breathe: A Mindfulness Curriculum for Adolescents to Cultivate Emotion Regulation, Attention, and Performance*
Brown, Creswell, and Ryan (Eds.) (2015)	*Handbook of Mindfulness*
Didonna (Ed.) (2009)	*Clinical Handbook of Mindfulness*
Gordon (1996)	*Manifesto for a New Medicine: Your Guide to Healing Partnerships and the Wise Use of Alternative Therapies*
Greco and Hayes (2008)	*Acceptance and Mindfulness Treatments for Children and Adolescents: A Practitioner's Guide*
Greenland (2010)	*The Mindful Child: How to Help Your Kid Manage Stress and Become Happier, Kinder, and More Compassionate*
Ie, Ngnoumen, and Langer (Eds.) (2014)	*The Wiley Blackwell Handbook of Mindfulness*
Kabat-Zinn (1990)	*Full Catastrophe Living: Using the Wisdom of Your Body and Mind to Face Stress, Pain and Illness*
Rechtschaffen (2014)	*The Way of Mindful Education: Cultivating Well-being in Teachers and Students*
Ryan (2012)	*A Mindful Nation: How a Simple Practice Can Help Us Reduce Stress, Improve Performance, and Recapture the American Spirit*
Saltzman (2014)	*A Still Quiet Place: A Mindfulness Program for Teaching Children and Adolescents to Ease Stress and Difficult Emotions*
Saltzman (2016)	*A Still Quiet Place for Teens: A Mindfulness Workbook to Ease Stress and Difficult Emotions*

(*continued*)

(continued)

	Websites
Benson-Henry Institute for Mind Body Medicine	http://www.bensonhenryinstitute.org
BHI: Resilient Schools Program	http://www.bensonhenryinstitute.org/services/resilient-schools
Center for Mind-Body Medicine	https://cmbm.org
Center for Mindfulness in Medicine, Healthcare, and Society (CFM)	http://www.umassmed.edu/cfm/
CFM: Mindfulness and Stress Reduction Clinic	http://www.umassmed.edu/cfm/stress-reduction/
David Lynch Foundation (TM)	https://www.davidlynchfoundation.org
TM	http://www.tm.org

References

Arnett, J. J. (1999). Adolescent storm and stress, reconsidered. *American Psychologist, 54*(5), 317–326.

Arnett, J. J. (2000). Emerging adulthood: A theory of development from the late teens through the twenties. *American Psychologist, 55*(5), 469–480.

Baer, R. A. (2003). Mindfulness training as a clinical intervention: A conceptual and empirical review. *Clinical Psychology: Science and Practice, 10*(2), 125–143.

Bakan, D. (1971). Adolescence in America: From idea to social fact. *Daedalus, 100*(4), 979–995. Retrieved from http://www.jstor.org/stable/20024043

Barnes, V. A., Treiber, F. A., & Davis, H. C. (2001). Impact of Transcendental Meditation on cardiovascular function at rest and during acute stress in adolescents with normal blood pressure. *Journal of Psychosomatic Research, 51*(4), 597–605.

Barnes, V. A., Bauza, L. B., & Treiber, F. A. (2003). Impact of stress reduction on negative school behavior in adolescents. *Health and Quality of Life Outcome, 1*(10). DOI:10.1186/1477-7525-1-10.

Barnes, V. A., Davis, H. C., Murzynowski, J. B., & Treiber, F. A. (2004). Impact of meditation on resting and ambulatory blood pressure and heart rate in youth. *Psychosomatic Medicine, 66*(6), 909–914.

Barnes, V. A., Treiber, F. A., & Johnson, M. H. (2004). Impact of Transcendental Meditation on ambulatory blood pressure in African American adolescents. *American Journal of Hypertension, 17*(4), 366–369.

Beauchemin, J., Hutchins, T. L., & Patterson, F. (2008). Mindfulness meditation may lessen anxiety, promote social skills, and improve academic performance among adolescents with learning disabilities. *Complementary Health Practice*

Review, 13; 34–45, retrieved June 22, 2009 from http://chp.sagepub.com/cgi/content/abstract/13/1/34.

Bendery, J. (2013). Amid the chaos of Capitol Hill, Tim Ryan offers reprieve with Quiet Time Caucus. Huffington Post. http://www.huffingtonpost.com/2013/07/25/tim-ryan-quiet-time-caucus_n_3653247.html?utm_hp_ref=third-metric&

Benson, H. (1975). *The Relaxation Response.* New York, NY: William Morrow.

Benson, H. (2000). *The Relaxation Response: 25th Anniversary edition.* New York, NY: Avon.

Benson, H. (2009). *Timeless Healing.* New York, NY: Simon and Schuster.

Benson, H., & Proctor, W. (2010). *Relaxation Revolution: The Science and Genetics of Mind Body Healing.* New York, NY: Simon and Schuster.

Benson, H., Kornhaber, A., Kornhaber, C., LeChanu, M. N., Zuttermeister, P. C., Myers, P., & Friedman, R. (1994). Increases in positive psychological characteristics with a new relaxation-response curriculum in high school students. *The Journal of Research and Development in Education, 27*(4), 226–231.

Benson, H., Wilcher, M., Greenberg, B., Higgins, E., Ennis, M., Zuttermeister, P. C., & Friedman, R. (2000). Academic performance among middle-school students after exposure to a relaxation response curriculum. *Journal of Research and Development in Education, 33*(3), 156–165.

Biegel, G. M. (2010). *The stress reduction workbook for teens: Mindfulness skills to help you deal with stress.* Oakland, CA: New Harbinger Publications.

Biegel, G. M, Brown, K. W., Shapiro, S. L, & Schubert, C. (2009). Mindfulness–based stress reduction for the treatment of adolescent psychiatric outpatients: A randomized clinical trial. *Journal of Clinical and Consulting Psychology, 77*(5), 855–866.

Bishop, S. R., Lau, M., Shapiro, S., Carlson, L., Anderson, N. D., Carmody, J., & Devins, G. (2004). Mindfulness: A proposed operational definition. *Clinical Psychology: Science and Practice, 11*(3), 230–241.

Black, D. S. (2015). Mindfulness training for children and adolescents: A state-of-the-science review. In K. W. Brown, R. M. Ryan, & J. D. Creswell (Eds.), *Handbook of mindfulness: Theory and research* (pp. 283–310). New York, NY: Guilford Press.

Black, D. S., Milam, J., & Sussman, S. (2009). Sitting-meditation interventions among youth: A review of treatment efficacy. *Pediatrics*, 124(3), 532–541.

Bloomfield, H. H., Cain, M. P., Jaffe, D. T., & Kory, R. B. (1975). *TM: Discovering Inner Energy and Overcoming Stress.* New York, NY: Dell Publishing.

Bogels, S., Hoogstad, B., Van Dun, L., De Shutter, S., & Restifo, K. (2008). Mindfulness training for adolescents with externalising disorders and their parents. *Behavioural and Cognitive Psychotherapy, 36*(2), 193–209.

Bootzin, R. R., & Stevens, S. J. (2005). Adolescents, substance abuse, and the treatment of insomnia and daytime sleepiness. *Clinical Psychology Review, 25*(5), 629–644.

Broderick, P. C. (2013). *Learning to Breathe: A Mindfulness Curriculum for Adolescents to Cultivate Emotion Regulation, Attention, and Performance.* Oakland, CA: New Harbinger Publications.

Brown, K. W., Creswell, J. D., & Ryan, R. M. (Eds.). (2015). *Handbook of mindfulness: Theory, research, and practice.* New York, NY: Guilford Publications.

Bryant, E. F. (2015). Hindu classical Yoga: Patanjali's Yoga Sutras. In L. Komjathy (Ed.) Contemplative literature: *A comparative sourcebook on meditation and contemplative prayer* (pp. 457–502). Albany, NY: State University of New York Press.

Burke, C.A. (2010). Mindfulness-based approaches with children and adolescents: A preliminary review of current research in an emergent field. *Journal of Child and Family Studies, 19*(2), 133–144.

Cogen, M. (2015). The Congressman on a quest to make America more Zen. New York Magazine. http://nymag.com/daily/intelligencer/2015/01/can-this-congressman-make-america-more-zen.html.

Cullen, M. (2011). Mindfulness-based interventions: An emerging phenomenon. *Mindfulness, 2*(3), 186–193.

Didonna, F. (2009). *Clinical handbook of mindfulness.* New York, NY: Springer.

Eberth, J., & Sedlmeier, P. (2012). The effects of mindfulness meditation: A meta-analysis. *Mindfulness, 3*(3), 174–189.

Erikson, E. H. (1968). *Identity: Youth and crisis.* New York, NY: Norton.

Esposito, J. L., Fasching, D. J., Lewis, T. T., & Bowlby, P. (2002). *World religions today.* New York, NY: Oxford University Press.

Felver, J. C., Celis-De Hoyos, C. E., Tezanos, K., & Singh, N. N. (2016). A systematic review of mindfulness-based interventions for youth in school settings. *Mindfulness, 7*(1), 34–45.

Gordon, J. S. (1996). *Manifesto for a new medicine: Your guide to healing partnerships and the wise use of alternative therapies.* Chicago: Da Capo Press.

Gordon, J. S., Staples, J. K., Blyta, A., & Bytyqi, M. (2004). Treatment of Posttraumatic Stress Disorder in postwar Kosovo high school students using mind-body skills groups: A pilot study. *Journal of Traumatic Stress, 17*(2), 143–147.

Goyal, M., Singh, S., Sibinga, E. M., Gould, N. F., Rowland-Seymour, A., Sharma, R., & Haythornthwaite, J. A. (2014). Meditation programs for psychological stress and well-being: a systematic review and meta-analysis. *JAMA Internal Medicine, 174*(3), 357–368.

Grabbe, L., Nguy, S. T., & Higgins, M. K. (2012). Spirituality development for homeless youth: A mindfulness meditation feasibility pilot. *Journal of Child and Family Studies, 21*(6), 925–937.

Greco, L. A., & Hayes, S. C. (2008). *Acceptance & mindfulness treatments for children & adolescents: A practitioner's guide.* Oakland, CA: New Harbinger Publications.

Greenland, S. K. (2010). *The mindful child: How to help your kid manage stress and become happier, kinder, and more compassionate.* New York, NY: Simon and Schuster.

Hall, G. S. (1904). *Adolescence: Its psychology and its relation to physiology, anthropology, sociology, sex, crime, religion, and education.* Englewood Cliffs, NJ: Prentice-Hall.

Hart, M. A. (2010). Indigenous worldviews, knowledge, and research: The development of an indigenous research paradigm. *Journal of Indigenous Voices in Social Work, 1*(1), 1–16.

Hollenstein, T., & Lougheed, J. P. (2013). Beyond storm and stress: Typicality, transactions, timing, and temperament to account for adolescent change. *American Psychologist, 68*(6), 444–454.

Hwang, W. C. (2011). Cultural adaptations: A complex interplay between clinical and cultural issues. *Clinical Psychology: Science and Practice, 18*(3), 238–241.

Ie, A., Ngnoumen, C. T., & Langer, E. J. (Eds.). (2014). *The Wiley Blackwell handbook of mindfulness.* West Sussex, UK: John Wiley & Sons.

Kabat-Zinn J. (1990). *Full catastrophe living: Using the wisdom of your body and mind to face stress, pain and illness.* New York, NY: Delacorte.

Kabat-Zinn, J. (2003). Mindfulness-based interventions in context: Past, present, and future. *Clinical Psychology: Science and Practice, 10*(2), 144–156.

Kabat-Zinn, J. (2011). Some reflections on the origins of MBSR, skillful means, and the trouble with maps. *Contemporary Buddhism, 12*(01), 281–306.

Keating, T. (1988). *Centering prayer.* Chicago, IL: Liturgical Press.

Khoury, B., Lecomte, T., Fortin, G., Masse, M., Therien, P., Bouchard, V., & Hofmann, S. G. (2013). Mindfulness-based therapy: A comprehensive meta-analysis. *Clinical Psychology Review, 33*(6), 763–771.

Komjathy, L. (2015). (Ed.) *Contemplative literature: A comparative sourcebook on meditation and contemplative prayer* (pp. 457–502). Albany, NY: State University of New York Press.

Lutz, A., Slagter, H. A., Dunne, J. D., & Davidson, R. J. (2008). Attention regulation and monitoring in meditation. *Trends in Cognitive Sciences, 12*(4), 163–169. DOI:10.1016/j.tics.2008.01.005

Magid, S. (2015). Jewish Kabbalah: Hayyim Vital's *Shaarei Kedusha.* In L. Komjathy (Ed.). *Contemplative literature: A comparative sourcebook on meditation and contemplative prayer* (pp. 197–264). Albany, NY: State University of New York Press.

Nash, J. D. & Newberg, A. B. (2013). *Toward a unifying taxonomy and definition for meditation.* Jefferson Myrna Brind Center of Integration Medicine Faculty Papers. Paper 11. http://jdc.jefferson.edu/jmbcimfp/11

Niemiec, R. M., Rashid, T., & Spinella, M. (2012). Strong mindfulness: Integrating mindfulness and character strengths. *Journal of Mental Health Counseling, 34*(3), 240.

Norton, C. L. (2011). *Innovative interventions in child and adolescent mental health.* New York, NY: Routledge.

Ospina, M. B., Bond, K., Karkhaneh, M., Tjosvold, L., Vandermeer, B., Liang, Y., & Klassen, T. P. (2007). *Meditation practices for health*: State of the research. In Evidence Report/Technology Assessment, 155, AHRQ Publication No. 07–E010. Edmonton, Alberta, Canada: University of Alberta Evidence-based Practice Center.

Parent, A. S., Teilmann, G., Juul, A., Skakkebaek, N. E., Toppari, J., & Bourguignon, J. P. (2003). The timing of normal puberty and the age limits of sexual precocity: Variations around the world, secular trends, and changes after migration. *Endocrine Reviews, 24*(5), 668–693.

Rawlett, K., & Scrandis, D. (2015). Mindfulness based programs implemented with at-risk adolescents. *Open Nursing Journal, 9*(1), 82–88.

Rechtschaffen, D. (2014). *The way of mindful education: Cultivating well-being in teachers and students.* New York, NY: WW Norton & Company.

Rosaen, C. & Benn, R. (2006). The experience of Transcendental Meditation in middle school students: A qualitative report. *Explore, 2*(5), 422–425.

Rosenthal, N. E. (2012). *Transcendence: Healing and transformation through Transcendental Meditation.* New York, NY: Tarcher/Penguin.

Roth, H. D. (2015). Daoist apophatic meditation: Selections from the classical Daoist textual corpus. In L. Komjathy (Ed.). *Contemplative literature: A comparative sourcebook on meditation and contemplative prayer* (pp. 89–144). Albany, NY: State University of New York Press.

Ryan, T. (2012). *A mindful nation: How a simple practice helps reduce stress, improve performance, and recapture the American spirit.* Carlsbad, CA: Hay House, Inc.

Saltzman, A. (2014). *A Still Quiet Place: A mindfulness program for teaching children and adolescents to ease stress and difficult emotions.* Oakland, CA: New Harbinger Publications.

Saltzman, A. (2016). *A Still Quiet Place for teens: A mindfulness workbook to ease stress and difficult emotions.* Oakland, CA: New Harbinger Publications.

Schoeberlein, D., & Koffler, T. (2005). *Garrison Institute report: Contemplation and education: A survey of programs using contemplative techniques in K–12 educational settings: A mapping report.* New York, NY: Garrison Institute.

Sedlmeier, P., Eberth, J., Schwarz, M., Zimmermann, D., Haarig, F., Jaeger, S., & Kunze, S. (2012). The psychological effects of meditation: A meta-analysis. *Psychological Bulletin, 138*(6), 1139.

Segal, Z. V., Williams, M. G., & Teasdale, J. D. (2002). *Mindfulness-based Cognitive Behavior Therapy for depression: A new approach to preventing relapse.* New York, NY: Guildford.

Singh, N. N., Lancioni, G. E., Singh Joy, S. D., Winton, A. S. W., Sabaawi, M., Wahler, R. G. & Singh, J. (2007). Adolescents with conduct disorder can be mindful of their aggressive behavior. *Journal of Emotional and Behavioral Disorders, 15*(1), 56–63.

Singh, N. N., Lancioni, G. E., Singh, A. N., Winton, A. S. W., Singh, J., McAleavey, K. M., & Adkins, A. D. (2008). A mindfulness-based health wellness program for an adolescent with Prader-Willi syndrome. *Behavior Modification, 32*(2), 167–181.

So, K., & Orme-Johnson, D. (2001). Three randomized experiments on the longitudinal effects of the Transcendental Meditation technique on cognition. *Intelligence, 29*, 419–440.

Spear, L. P. (2000). The adolescent brain and age-related behavioral manifestations. *Neuroscience & Biobehavioral Reviews, 24*(4), 417–463.

Teasdale, J. D., Segal, Z., & Williams, J. M. G. (1995). How does cognitive therapy prevent depressive relapse and why should attentional control (mindfulness) training help? *Behaviour Research and Therapy, 33*(1), 25–39.

Thomson, R. F. (2000). Zazen and psychotherapeutic presence. *American Journal of Psychotherapy, 54*(4), 531.

Vago, D. R. (2016). *Peer-reviewed research.* Retrieved March 10, 2016, 2016, from https://contemplativemind.wordpress.com/peer-reviewed-research-mindfulness-meditation-contemplative-practice/.

Wall, R. B. (2005). Tai Chi and mindfulness-based stress reduction in a Boston Middle School. *Journal of Pediatric Health Care, 19*(4), 230–237.

Wisner, B. L. (2008). *The impact of meditation as a cognitive-behavioral practice for alternative high school student* (Doctoral dissertation). ProQuest.

Wisner, B. L., Jones, B., & Gwin, D. (2010). School-based meditation practices for adolescents: A resource for strengthening self-regulation, emotional coping, and self-esteem. *Children & Schools, 32*(3), 150–159.

Wisner, B. L. (2014). An exploratory study of mindfulness meditation for alternative school students: Perceived benefits for improving school climate and student functioning. *Mindfulness, 5*(6), 626–638.

Wisner, B. L., & Norton, C. L. (2013). Capitalizing on behavioral and emotional strengths of alternative high school students through group counseling to promote mindfulness skills. *The Journal for Specialists in Group Work, 38*(3), 207–224.

Wisner, B. L., & Starzec, J. J. (2011). Meditative practices for children and adolescents. In C. L. Norton (Ed.), *Innovative interventions in child and adolescent mental health* (pp. 141–161). New York, NY: Routledge.

Wisner, B. L., & Starzec, J. J. (2016). The process of personal transformation for adolescents practicing mindfulness skills in an alternative school setting. *Child and Adolescent Social Work Journal, 33*(3), 245–257.

World Health Organization (2016). Adolescent development. Retrieved from http://www.who.int/maternal_child_adolescent/topics/adolescence/dev/en/

Zenner, C., Herrnleben–Kurz, S., & Walach, H. (2014). Mindfulness-based interventions in schools-a systematic review and meta-analysis. *Frontiers in Psychology*, *5*(603). DOI:10.3389/fpsyg.2014.00603

Zoogman, S., Goldberg, S. B., Hoyt, W. T., & Miller, L. (2015). Mindfulness interventions with youth: A meta-analysis. *Mindfulness*, *6*(2), 290–302.

Zylowska, L., Ackerman, D. L., Yang, M. H., Futrell, J. L., Horton, N. L., Hale, S.T., & Smalley, S. L. (2008). Mindfulness meditation training in adults and adolescents with ADHD: A feasibility study. *Journal of Attention Disorders*, *11* (6), 737–746.

CHAPTER 2

Theoretical Foundations Supporting Mindfulness and Meditation for Adolescents

Introduction

A solid and integrated theoretical foundation informs our work with adolescents; it provides a framework that helps us choose our actions and decisions when designing and providing mindfulness and meditation practices and programs for adolescents. In Chapter 1, pertinent concepts and important contributors to mindfulness and meditation practices and programs were discussed. In order to situate the application of this work with adolescents, this chapter offers an overview of theoretical contexts and contemporary theories relevant to understanding adolescent development and use of mindfulness and meditation practices for adolescents.

An integrative foundation to guide use of mindfulness and meditation practices with adolescents is particularly helpful for supporting these programs in various settings, including schools, counseling agencies, hospitals, and communities. Many theoretical perspectives are likely to be incorporated in this work; however, only those that most closely pertain to secular mindfulness and meditation practices for adolescents are discussed here. These include perspectives on the functions of meditation, developmental neuroscience, cognitive-behavioral theory, systems theory, and the Transtheoretical Model of Change (TTM: Prochaska & DiClemente, 1982).

Once these theoretical frameworks have been discussed, some of the perspectives that inform our understanding of the reason that mindfulness and meditation practices are particularly helpful to adolescents will be

B.L. Wisner, *Mindfulness and Meditation for Adolescents*,
DOI 10.1057/978-1-349-95207-6_2

explored. These include adolescent identity development, positive psychology, Positive Youth Development (PYD; Lerner et al., 2005), and the bio-psycho-social-cultural approach. These perspectives are particularly important for positioning the use of mindfulness and meditation practices in the context of adolescent development.

Theoretical Foundations of Mindfulness and Meditation

As mentioned in Chapter 1, secular meditation practices for adolescents are the methods most often addressed in the medical, mental health, and wellness literature. This is consistent with the view of meditation as a means to self-regulation (to overcome psychological or emotional problems) in Western theoretical approaches, and contrasts with Buddhist and Hindu (i.e., Eastern) theoretical approaches that view meditation as a means to transform consciousness (Sedlmeier et al., 2012).

There are efforts to combine these two approaches; one example of this is a model proposed by Wallace and Shapiro (2006). This model combines Buddhist approaches to "mental development" with Western secular models of "health and well-being" (p. 699). In this approach wellness is achieved through development of conative, attentional, cognitive, and affective mental balance. In this model, conative balance is the ability to set priorities, achieve goals, and prioritize actions. Conative balance precedes the other three types of mental balance (i.e., attentional, cognitive, and affective balance). Thus, attention, thoughts, emotions, and setting goals and priorities support a successful mindfulness or meditation practice and contribute to wellness.

Some theoretical models prioritize the role of attentional control in meditation and the consequent benefits of emotional self-regulation (Lutz, Slagter, Dunne, & Davidson, 2008), while other models specifically target a variety of mechanisms underlying mindfulness practices (Baer, 2003; Baer, Smith, Hopkins, Krietemeyer, & Toney, 2006; Brown, Ryan, & Creswell, 2007; Shapiro, Carlson, Astin, & Freedman, 2006). Hölzel, Lazar et al. (2011) addressed these mechanisms and incorporated neuroscience in their comprehensive theoretical framework to explain how mindfulness meditation works. They also reviewed the empirical research on mindfulness meditation with adult participants and integrated the findings into their theory. They proposed that mindfulness meditation exerts its effects through the components of attention regulation, body awareness, emotion regulation, and changes in perspectives on the self (Hölzel, Lazar et al., 2011).

Mechanisms of mindfulness also are discussed by Vago and Silbersweig (2012) in their S-ART framework. In this framework, mindfulness is a broad concept that encompasses "perceptual, physiological, cognitive, emotional, and behavioral component processes" (p. 2). According to the S-ART model, mindfulness increases self-awareness (i.e., meta-awareness), self-regulation (i.e., ability to modulate one's behavior), and prosocial characteristics (i.e., self-transcendence). Vago and Silbersweig (2012) contend that mindfulness practice (i.e., "mental training") brings about changes in the brain (p. 2). Thus, the authors discuss mechanisms that support mindfulness in the following quote:

> In support of S-ART, six neurocognitive component mechanisms that are highly integrated and strengthened together through intentional mental strategies underlying the practice and cultivation of mindfulness are proposed to modulate networks of self-processing and reduce bias. These mechanisms include intention and motivation, attention and emotion regulation, extinction and reconsolidation, prosociality, non-attachment, and de-centering.

Clearly, themes related to intrapersonal and interpersonal mechanisms are evident in these diverse approaches. These efforts toward understanding the mechanisms of meditation and mindfulness will support development of more precise research and will provide a more solid theoretical base to support findings. This will help researchers to identify potential mismatches in the measures used in meditation studies and will support the progress of meditation research (Sedlmeier et al., 2012; Shear, 2006).

This highlights the importance of incorporating appropriate theoretical contexts when designing services for adolescents and when conducting research with adolescents. However, since theories of meditation are based on adults, it isn't clear how the theories would be adapted for application to adolescents. Efforts to clarify these factors entail exploring relevant theoretical contexts related to mindfulness and meditation programs for adolescents. One of these perspectives is developmental neuroscience, a discipline that has relevance for understanding how practicing mindfulness and meditation brings about physiological changes in the brain and behavior.

Placing Meditation in Context: Theoretical Frameworks

Growth and Development in Adolescence: The Role of Developmental Neuroscience

In Chapter 1, adolescence was defined as a unique stage of development ranging from ages 10–18 or 19 (Arnett, 2000; World Health Organization, 2016). Adolescence is a time of rapid and extensive physiological development involving growth in height and weight, sexual maturation, and brain development (Forbes, & Dahl, 2010). Developmental neuroscience, the study of brain development across the lifespan, guides our understanding of connections between brain maturation and cognition, emotions, and behavior. Neural development in childhood and adolescence contains periods of rapid growth followed by episodes of synaptic refinement and pruning (Lerner, Lamb, & Freund, 2010). Neural development is related to attention, executive functioning, and self-regulation (Rueda, Posner, & Rothbart, 2005). In addition, it is now well-established through advances in research, that neural development continues throughout adolescence and into emerging adulthood (Taber-Thomas, & Perez-Edgar, 2015). Developmental neuroscience research with adolescent participants is quickly expanding with studies exploring typical brain development as well as brain development in those with mental health and developmental challenges (Pfeifer & Blakemore, 2012; Sowell, Trauner, Gamst, & Jernigan, 2002).

Processes of attention, comprised of alerting, orienting, and executive aspects, serve as a foundation for awareness and self-regulation (Posner & Rothbart, 2007). Self-regulation may be viewed as the ability to manage thoughts, feelings, and behaviors in the context of effort and motivational factors and is promoted through executive functioning (Hofmann, Schmeichel, & Baddeley, 2012). These efforts toward self-regulation are particularly associated with growth of the prefrontal cortex (Banfield, Wyland, Macrae, Münte, & Heatherton, 2004). Executive functioning has been described as an aspect of cognition involving "higher-level" functions such as inhibition, use of working memory, and regulation of behavior directed toward attaining goals (Alvarez & Emory, 2006, p. 17).

Steinberg (2005) suggests that changes in brain structure and function in adolescence are related to abilities to control responses, weigh risks versus rewards for behaviors, and regulation of emotion. Especially notable, for our purposes, are developments within the prefrontal cortex, communication between the prefrontal cortex and various parts of the brain, development of cognitive abilities, and behavioral flexibility (Steinberg, 2005).

Research has substantiated that engaging in meditation practices changes brain structure and function for adult participants. This is true for changes in neural areas related to attention, executive function, and self-regulation. For example, use of mindfulness-based practices is related to changes in the left-sided anterior activation on electroencephalogram (EEG) readings (Davidson et al., 2003), magnetic resonance imaging (MRI) readings in the right anterior dorsal insula (Luders et al., 2012), MRI readings in the posterior cingulate cortex, the temporo-parietal junction, and the cerebellum (Hölzel, Carmody et al., 2011), and diffusion tensor imaging (DTI) readings in the anterior cingulate cortex (Tang, Lu, Fan, Yang, & Posner, 2012). Similarly, findings for practitioners of the relaxation response showed changes in the dorsolateral prefrontal and parietal cortices, hippocampus/para hippocampus, temporal lobe, pregenual anterior cingulate cortex, striatum, and pre- and post-central gyri on functional magnetic resonance imaging (Lazar, Bush, Gollub, Fricchione, Khalsa, & Benson, 2000). In addition, EEG readings revealed changes in alpha activity, brain wave coherence, and neural activation during Transcendental Meditation (Travis et al., 2010). Research is needed that establishes similar findings in adolescents exposed to mindfulness and meditation programs (Sanger & Dorjee, 2015).

Developmental neuroscience is a biologically based theory that helps us understand adolescent behavior. We can provide a broader theoretical base from which to understand behavior by incorporating psychological theories such as cognitive-behavioral theory.

Cognitive-Behavioral Theory: The Role of Thoughts and Behavior

The cognitive-behavioral theory explains human functioning through the lenses of cognitive features and behavioral aspects. The cognitive perspective encompasses perception and information processing, while the behavioral perspective encompasses learning theories (Payne, 2014). As mentioned, the cognitive mechanisms related to attention provide the foundation for self-awareness and the ability to regulate thoughts and emotions (Posner & Rothbart, 2007).

Prochaska and Norcross (2007) define cognitive-behavioral therapy as the use of cognitive techniques and explanations in order to bring about behavioral change. In cognitive therapy clients are encouraged to attend to the present as opposed to the past and to monitor thinking in order to identify negative thoughts and feelings or behaviors. In this manner, irrational thought patterns may be altered (Beck, Rush, Shaw, & Emery, 1979). Initially, cognitive-behavioral techniques were developed to treat depression, but they have been adapted to treat many other concerns such as panic and anxiety disorders, post-traumatic stress disorder, and eating disorders (Hollon & Beck, 2004).

Meditation may be viewed through the lens of cognitive-behavioral theory and therapy since meditation as an intervention has its basis in cognition (Keefe, 1996). Meditation is sometimes considered an exercise for the mind, a way to become familiar with how we think or the process of thought. In this sense, meditation is a cognitive practice. This connection is exemplified by the following "Adolescent Voices" quote in which a high school student describes how meditation helped her modify her behavior through a cognitive-behavioral process.

Adolescent Voices

"Meditation helps me take time to stand back and think before reacting."

Adolescent Mindfulness Meditation Practitioner
(Wisner, 2014, p. 633)

Cognitive-behavioral theory is particularly relevant to the cognitive-directed methods of meditation (e.g., Tai Chi Chuan and mindfulness) as described by Nash and Newberg (2013). Cognitive-behavioral theory, in concert with knowledge of brain structure and function, helps us understand how the cognitive and behavioral components of meditation work and how these practices may be implemented. This information provides a strong impetus for using these practices with adolescents, especially where the aim is to help them modify some aspect of current behavioral or cognitive functioning.

The biological basis of developmental neuroscience and the psychological aspects of cognitive-behavioral theory are important. However, compartmentalizing these areas of development and failing to consider the whole person should be avoided. This concern may be addressed by considering the broader perspectives of systems and ecological theories applicable to work with adolescents.

Systems and Ecological Theories: Placing Development in a Holistic Context

Payne (2014), in a discussion of systems and ecological perspectives, suggested that systems views are important since these views go beyond the individual and address broader social concerns. The individual is viewed as a complex system interacting with other complex systems; thus, there is a reciprocal interaction between systems in the context of a person's life. The systems theoretical approach asserts that when an individual makes personal changes, the systems within which the individual operates are also likely to undergo change (Prochaska & Norcross, 2007).

One of the major systems perspectives related to adolescence is Erik Erikson's (1968) psychosocial approach. This perspective (a combination of psychoanalytic theory and systems concepts) contributed to understanding development across the lifespan and helped to clarify the developmental tasks occurring in each stage of life. Erikson emphasized that each stage of the lifespan presented new opportunities for growth and development, with the primary developmental task of adolescence being engagement in the identity formation process.

Erikson's psychosocial approach provided a clear departure from historical views of development which emphasized biologically based theories. While he recognized the importance of biological factors in development, he also considered social and cultural factors important in development. A comprehensive discussion of Erikson's work and seminal contributions may be found elsewhere (Stevens, 2008).

The psychosocial model was adapted and expanded for use in clinical and medical settings such as the biopsychosocial model in the field of medicine (Engel, 1977), and the bio-psycho-social-cultural model in the mental health field (Rosen, 2006). Systems theories have also been applied in family therapy settings (Payne, 2014) and ecological theories guide social work in various practice settings through the Life Model of Social Work Practice (Gitterman & Germain, 2008).

One of the most widely known ecological theories is the bio-ecological systems perspective developed by Urie Bronfenbrenner and elaborated upon by Bronfenbrenner and his colleagues (Bronfenbrenner, 1977; Bronfenbrenner & Ceci, 1994; Bronfenbrenner & Crouter, 1983; Bronfenbrenner & Morris, 1998). In this theory, individual development is considered within a nested contextual framework exemplified by the Process-Person-Context-Time Model (Bronfenbrenner, 2005; Tudge,

Mokrova, Hatfield & Karnik, 2009). In this model, an individual's unique biological, behavioral, cognitive, and emotional characteristics contribute to the process of development within environmental, social, and historical contexts. Aspects of the environment include the microsystem, mesosystem, exosystem, and macrosystem (Bronfenbrenner, 2005).

In the microsystem, the individual experiences roles and relationships within particular settings such as home and school. The mesosystem involves links between settings within the microsystem. An example of this would be a parent-teacher conference scheduled to make sure a student has the family and school support needed to succeed academically. The exosystem includes links between settings within the microsystem and another system in which the individual typically does not interact. An example of this for an adolescent may be the parent's workplace. While the adolescent does not necessarily spend time at the workplace, the parent's behavior toward the adolescent may vary due to events occurring in the workplace. The macrosystem includes the wider contexts exemplified by the culture in which the individual lives. In addition to these contexts, the model also incorporates factors of time, including the time of life that the individual is currently experiencing, the family historical factors, and the wider historical contexts within the culture or society (Bronfenbrenner, 2005).

Contextual factors such as these play an important role in meditation practice (Lutz et al., 2008). The systems and ecological frameworks offer a holistic approach for understanding these contextual factors and are particularly relevant when discussing meditation practices that evolved from the field of mind-body medicine. Shapiro and Schwartz (2000) recognize the importance of the systemic perspective in understanding the potential benefits of mindfulness practices. Their model of intentional systemic mindfulness (ISM) connects the qualities of mindfulness with the systemic perspectives that influence the use of mindfulness. This perspective also highlights the connection of a mindfulness practice to self-regulation.

An example of systems influences in meditation research may be seen in a study conducted with alternative high school students (Wisner, 2014). In this study, students described changes in the student community that they attributed to the mindfulness meditation program. These systemic changes are reflected in the following "Adolescent Voices" quote, in which a high school student speaks of the changes he observed in the wider school community. He believed that the school environment changed in a positive way after the meditation program. Thus, consistent with the systemic perspective, when students make changes in thoughts, emotions, and behaviors, there are corresponding changes in relationships with classmates, friends, teachers, parents, and other family members.

Adolescent Voices

"Meditation has had a positive impact on our school, it has made a better school environment and gave people a way to calm down without flipping out."

Adolescent Mindfulness Meditation Practitioner
(Wisner, 2014, p. 633)

Other theories have been developed to help us understand what happens as people change some aspect of their behavior. For example, the transtheoretical model of change (Prochaska & DiClemente, 1982) provides a general theory of behavior change that clarifies what happens as people engage in efforts to modify behavior.

The Transtheoretical Model of Change: Supporting Change through Integrative Practice

The transtheoretical model of change (TTM) offers a way of understanding how people change their behavior by integrating principles from various psychological, psychotherapeutic, and learning perspectives (Prochaska & DiClemente, 1982; Prochaska & Velicer, 1997). The TTM identifies five stages of change and ten processes of change. The model also addresses pros and cons of changing, self-efficacy (i.e., confidence that change can be sustained), and temptation to engage in a behavior that the person is trying to change or eliminate (Prochaska & DiClemente, 1982; Prochaska, Redding, & Evers, 2008).

The stages that people move through as they work toward change include Precontemplation (i.e., lack of intention to take action in the near future), Contemplation, (i.e., action is planned), Preparation (i.e., behavioral steps toward action are taken), Action (i.e., behavior change), Maintenance (i.e., behavior change continues), and Termination (i.e., confidence in continuation of behavior change). Ten common activities are used to progress through these stages (Prochaska et al., 2008, p. 99). These are called the processes of change and they include:

- *consciousness raising* for increasing awareness,
- *dramatic relief* through uncomfortable emotions about unhealthy behavior,

- *self-reevaluation* through imagining change as an aspect of the self,
- *environmental reevaluation* through understanding how personal behavior impacts social and environmental factors,
- *self-liberation* related to believing in and committing to change,
- engaging *helping relationships* to support health-related behavior change,
- *counterconditioning* resulting in learning healthier behaviors,
- *reinforcement management* through selective rewards for behavior,
- moderating *stimulus control* through selective cues for promoting or decreasing habits, and
- *social liberation* through optimizing knowledge of societal support for wellness.

The TTM provides useful guidance when planning and instituting intervention programs. Examples of these diverse programs include those designed to help people stop smoking, manage alcohol abuse, lose weight, and manage stress (Prochaska et al., 2008). The TTM principles and activities could also be adapted for use while designing secular meditation programs, particularly those that target self-regulation. For instance, Prochaska and Velicer (1997) suggested that TTM principles may be used to match interventions to the particular stage of change that the individual is experiencing. The following "Adolescent Voices" quote illustrates these principles. The student's journal entry tells us that she has progressed in her meditation practice. She realizes when she "gets off track" and can bring herself back to the meditation practice. Someone experiencing this is engaging in self-regulation and would benefit from more advanced instruction to support the progress. The processes of change in the TTM, such as self-reevaluation, environmental reevaluation, and moderating stimulus control are relevant in these circumstances.

Adolescent Voices

"The time spent with meditation is a nice quiet time for me, I don't have to worry about anything. I just sit there and concentrate on my breathing, sometimes I get off track but when I realize that I'm off track, I bring myself back in and concentrate on my breathing again."

Adolescent Mindfulness Meditation Practitioner
(Wisner, 2013, p. 55)

Discussion of these factors in the TTM also highlights the importance of timing when offering mindfulness and meditation practices to adolescents. Given the wide range of changes that occur in response to mindfulness and meditation practices, the role of the TTM will be explored in more detail in the discussion of teaching mindfulness and meditation to adolescents in Chapter 7.

While these theoretical frameworks provide a foundation from which to understand how to use mindfulness and meditation with adolescents, it is also important to address factors directly related to adolescent growth and development. These contexts include adolescent identity development, positive psychology, and positive youth development.

Adolescent Development in Context

Adolescent Identity Development

Previous discussion included an overview of contemporary adolescent development with relevant historical factors, including Erik Erikson's views of lifespan development (1968; 1982). In this framework, the primary task facing adolescents is formation of a unique sense of self, and a sense of identity that evolves over time. Erikson maintained that cognitive, social, and cultural factors are crucial for facilitating the adolescent identity development process. This identity includes formation of a personal identity and recognition of belongingness within a particular group (Erikson, 1968; Stevens, 2008). While this identity development process was once considered to involve a crisis of sorts (Erikson, 1968), it is now viewed as a developmental task that may or may not involve an identity crisis (Marcia, 1966). Thus, while not all adolescents struggle during this identity process, for some adolescents the process is marked by some level of struggle or crisis (Marcia, 1966; Meeus, Iedema, Helsen, & Vollebergh, 1999). When we do encounter adolescents who experience challenges in adolescence, it is important to provide these youth with extra assistance in order to maximize their cognitive, social, and emotional potential for growth.

James Marcia's ego identity status model (Marcia, 1966; 1980; Marcia, Waterman, Matteson, Archer, & Orlofsky, 1993) expands on Erikson's ideas about adolescent identity development. Consistent with Erikson's theory, identity development occurs throughout the lifespan and changes in identity may occur in response to life events (Erikson, 1968; Stephen, Fraser, & Marcia, 1992). By assessing an individual on two independent processes (i.e., exploration of personal identity issues and commitment to personal beliefs in areas related to work, ideology, and relationships), an individual may be categorized within one of four different identity statuses. These statuses include identity achievement, identity moratorium, identity foreclosure, and identity diffusion (Marcia, 1980; Marcia et al., 1993).

Identity achievement is marked by a firm level of commitment to work, ideology, and intimate relationships following personal exploration of ideas about these areas. Identity moratorium involves an active identity exploration process, but the individual lacks a firm personal commitment to work, ideology, and intimate relationships. An individual in identity foreclosure has a firm sense of commitment to work, ideology, and intimate relationships, but this occurs without having engaged in an active exploration process. The final status is identity diffusion which is characterized by the absence of firm commitment to work, ideology, and intimate relationships and may occur with or without exploration (Marcia et al., 1993).

Early in the identity process, adolescents are more likely to fit into the diffusion status (i.e., the absence of significant sense of personal identity) or the foreclosure status (i.e., commitment to ideas and values adopted from respected people in the absence of active exploration of identity) (Stephen, Fraser, & Marcia, 1992). As such, the number of adolescents in foreclosure and diffusion decline with the move into late adolescence and young adulthood (Kroger, Martinussen, & Marcia, 2010). These individuals are more likely to continue with active exploration of ideas about work, ideology, and intimate relationships without a firm commitment (i e., the moratorium status) or with identity commitment exemplified by personal exploration of identity related to relationships, vocation, and ideologies (Stephen et al., 1992). Although identity achievement is more likely to occur in adolescents as they progress through late adolescence and young adulthood, many individuals have not reached identity achievement by the end of adolescence (Kroger, Martinussen, & Marcia, 2010).

A salient aspect of adolescent identity involves ethnic identity development which is dynamic and changes over time. Ethnic identity involves a shared sense of identity and sense of belongingness to an ethnic group (French, Seidman, Allen, & Aber, 2006; Phinney & Ong, 2007). Consistent with

Marcia's identity status model (Marcia et al., 1993), an individual's ethnic identity may reflect one of four statuses. These are diffusion status (i.e., lack of a clear ethnic identity), foreclosure status (i.e., commitment to an ethnic identity without engaging in an active exploration of this identity), moratorium (i.e., an active exploration of ethnicity but no commitment to an ethnic identity), or ethnic identity achievement (i.e., a firm commitment to one's ethnicity based on an active exploration process) (Phinney & Ong, 2007, p. 275). Additional discussion of ethnic and racial identity development models may be found in the literature about particular populations including African Americans (Cross & Fhagen-Smith, 2001; Cross, Strauss, & Fhagen-Smith, 1999; Helms, 1990; 2007), Hispanics and Latinos (Arce, 1981; Organista, 2007; Umana-Taylor, Vargas-Chanes, Garcia, & Gonzales-Backen, 2008), European Americans (e.g., Helms, 1990; 2007), Asian Americans (e.g., Yeh & Huang, 1996), and American Indians/First Nations (e.g., Byers, 2005; Jones & Galliher, 2007).

When using mindfulness and meditation with adolescents, addressing factors such as identity development and ethnicity supports culturally sensitive and developmentally appropriate practices and programs (e.g., Fung, Guo, Jin, Bear & Lau, 2016; Hinton, Pich, Hofmann, & Otto, 2013). As reflected in the following "Adolescent Voices" quote, meditation provides an opportunity to connect with ourselves and explore who we are. This is important for adolescents who often spend little time in an environment conducive to calming the mind and exploring the self in this manner. In this context, meditation may provide support for identity development and offer an opportunity to develop a sense of belongingness.

Adolescent Voices

"I've noticed when I'm at peace with myself for the short period of time, I actually work up some things that will make me think about who I am and what really matters to me in my life."

Adolescent Mindfulness Meditation Practitioner
(Wisner, 2013, p. 55)

Identity factors may also contribute to whether or not adolescents are interested in learning mindfulness and meditation practices. Many people have misconceptions about meditation, and this may contribute to the idea that meditation is not a practice that would appeal to them. This is reflected in the following "Adolescent Voices" quote by a mindfulness meditation participant who describes her initial reactions to the idea of trying meditation in a school-based program. The student went on to fully engage in the mindfulness practices offered in the program and eventually found benefit in her participation.

Adolescent Voices

"I personally thought negative things about it [meditation].
I thought it was the TV cliché.
Where everyone sits in a goofy position and closes their eyes and hums."

Adolescent Mindfulness Meditation Practitioner
(Wisner, 2013, p. 58)

Positive Psychology and Positive Youth Development
Much of the psychological literature about adolescents, as with adults, has been oriented toward recognizing, assessing, and treating problems. In contrast, recent efforts strive to recognize the possibilities of studying and facilitating more positive aspects of development through positive psychology. Seligman and Csikszentmihalyi (2000) predicted that, "a psychology of positive human functioning will arise that achieves a scientific understanding and effective interventions to build thriving in individuals, families and communities" (p. 13). Since that time the field of positive psychology has yielded a wide range of studies of positive functioning across the lifespan.

The success of positive psychology for adolescents has been corroborated through research in positive youth development (Lerner et al., 2005). Programs that involve positive youth development (PYD) often promote self-efficacy and resilience with increases in social, emotional, cognitive, behavioral, and moral competence. These programs often foster self-determination and positive identity for youth (Catalano, Berglund, Ryan, Lonczak, & Hawkins, 2004).

Positive youth development is consistent with efforts toward maximizing social support and internal strengths and minimizing deficits and high-risk behaviors (Benson, Scales, Leffert, & Roehlkepartain, 1999). Larson (2000) specifically addresses the importance of this approach in his discussion of literature related to how adolescents spend their time and how to maximize positive effects on youth development. There also are indications that strengths-based programs for youth that are consistent with PYD promote competence, confidence, character, connection, and caring in adolescents.

These strengths are referred to as the 5 Cs of PYD (Lerner et al., 2005; Roth & Brooks-Gunn, 2003). Lerner (2004) emphasized that programs most likely to result in the development of the 5-Cs of PYD offer opportunities for adolescents to form relationships with supportive adults, to engage in activities that build skills, and provide opportunities for youth to participate in activities in the community. These aspects of PYD promote thriving and healthy development in young people within the context of a hopeful future embedded in personal and societal relationships (Lerner, 2004). Positive youth development also may be related to spiritual and religious factors that promote thriving in youth (Lerner, 2004).

Positive youth development also is related to promotion of developmental assets within personal, family, and community contexts. These assets include external assets of support, empowerment, boundaries and expectations, and constructive use of time. Internal assets include commitment to learning, positive values, social competencies, and positive identity (Benson, Scales, Leffert, & Roehlkepartain, 1999).

Mindfulness and meditation programs have been shown to promote the 5 Cs of PYD and these programs help adolescents develop personal strengths and find alternatives to high-risk behavior patterns (Black, 2015; Bootzin, & Stevens, 2005; Sharp, Niemiec, & Lawrence, 2016; Wisner & Norton, 2013). The potential of mindfulness skills to support personal strengths is illustrated by the following "Adolescent Voices" quote.

Adolescent Voices

"The changes for me I've noticed about myself while doing the meditation would be a more positive attitude. Meditation was a big part in the fact that my self-esteem went up."

Adolescent Mindfulness Meditation Practitioner
(Wisner, 2013, p. 54)

Summary

Why does mindfulness and meditation help adolescents? The answer may be found in understanding the relevant theoretical foundations underlying both adolescent development and mindfulness and meditation practices. Knowledge of developmental neuroscience and cognitive-behavioral theory helps us understand the neurological and cognitive changes that occur when adolescents meditate. In addition, understanding the systems and ecological perspectives provides a context for explaining the importance of environmental and social support for adolescents who participate in these programs.

When developing mindfulness and meditation programs for youth, knowledge of the transtheoretical model of change can inform decisions about the timing of interventions and program delivery. Likewise, knowledge of identity development and positive youth development can guide decisions about offering particular practices and programs and how to maximize program elements to promote adolescent strengths.

The quality of mindfulness and meditation programs offered to adolescents is strengthened by incorporating theory into program development. With these factors in mind, the next chapter provides a comprehensive synthesis of the research on mindfulness and meditation practices and programs for adolescents.

References

Alvarez, J. A., & Emory, E. (2006). Executive function and the frontal lobes: A meta-analytic review. *Neuropsychology Review, 16*(1), 17–42.

Arce, C. H. (1981). Reconsideration of Chicano culture and identity. *Daedalus, 110*, 177–191.

Arnett, J. J. (2000). Emerging adulthood: A theory of development from the late teens through the twenties. *American Psychologist, 55*(5), 469–480.

Baer, R. A. (2003). Mindfulness training as a clinical intervention: A conceptual and empirical review. *Clinical Psychology: Science and Practice, 10*(2), 125–143.

Baer, R. A., Smith, G. T., Hopkins, J., Krietemeyer, J., & Toney, L. (2006). Using self-report assessment methods to explore facets of mindfulness. *Assessment, 13* (1), 27–45.

Banfield, J. F., Wyland, C. L., Macrae, C. N., Münte, T. F., & Heatherton, T. F. (2004). The cognitive neuroscience of self-regulation. In R. F. Baumeister & K. D. Vohs, (Eds.), *Handbook of self-regulation: Research, theory, and applications* (pp. 62–83). New York, NY: Guilford.

Beck, A. T., Rush, A. J., Shaw, B. F., & Emery, G. (1979). Cognitive therapy of depression. *New York, NY: Guilford.*

Benson, P. L., Scales, P. C., Leffert, N., & Roehlkepartain, E. C. (1999). *A fragile foundation: The state of developmental assets among American youth.* Minneapolis, MN: Search Institute.

Black, D. S. (2015). p: A state-of-the-science review. In K. W. Brown, R. M. Ryan, & J. D. Creswell (Eds.), *Handbook of mindfulness: Theory and research* (pp. 283–310). New York, NY: Guilford Press.

Bootzin, R. R., & Stevens, S. J. (2005). Adolescents, substance abuse, and the treatment of insomnia and daytime sleepiness. *Clinical Psychology Review*, *25* (5), 629–644.

Bronfenbrenner, U. (1977). Toward an experimental ecology of human development. *American Psychologist*, *32*(7), 513–531.

Bronfenbrenner, U. (2005). *Making human beings human: Bioecological perspectives on human development.* Thousand Oaks, CA: Sage Publications.

Bronfenbrenner, U., & Ceci, S. J. (1994). Nature-nurture reconceptualized in developmental perspective: A bioecological model. *Psychological Review*, *101*(4), 568.

Bronfenbrenner, U., & Crouter, A. C. (1983). The evolution of environmental models in developmental research. In P. H. Mussen (Series Ed.) & W. Kessen (Vol. Ed.). *Handbook of child psychology, Volume 1. History, Theory, and Methods* (4th ed., pp. 357–414). New York, NY: John Wiley.

Bronfenbrenner, U., & Morris, P. A. (1998). The ecology of developmental processes. In W. Damon (Series Ed.) &, R. M. Lerner (Vol. Ed.). *Handbook of child psychology: Volume 1: Theoretical models of human development* (5th ed., pp. 993–1028). Hoboken, NJ: John Wiley.

Brown, K. W., Ryan, R. M., & Creswell, J. D. (2007). Mindfulness: Theoretical foundations and evidence for its salutary effects. *Psychological Inquiry*, *18*(4), 211–237.

Byers, L. G. (2005). Depression, discrimination, trauma, and American Indian ethnic identity (Unpublished doctoral dissertation), Washington University, Saint Louis, MO.

Catalano, R. F., Berglund, M. L., Ryan, J. A., Lonczak, H. S., & Hawkins, J. D. (2004). Positive youth development in the United States: Research findings on evaluations of positive youth development programs. *The Annals of the American Academy of Political and Social Science*, *591*(1), 98–124.

Cross, W., & Fhagen-Smith, P. (2001). Patterns of African American identity development: A Life span perspective. In C. Wijeyesinghe & B. Jackson, III (Eds.), *New perspectives on Racial Identity Development: A theoretical and practical anthology* (pp. 243–270). New York, NY: New York University Press.

Cross, W. E., Strauss, L., & Fhagen-Smith, P. (1999). African American identity development across the life span: Educational implications. In R. H. Sheets & E. R. Hollins (Eds.), *Racial and ethnic identity in school practices: Aspects of human development* (pp. 29–47). Mahwah, NJ: Erlbaum.

Davidson, R. J., Kabat-Zinn, J., Schumacher, J., Rosenkranz, M., Muller, D., Santorelli, S. F., & Sheridan, J. F. (2003). Alterations in brain and immune function produced by mindfulness meditation. *Psychosomatic Medicine*, *65*(4), 564–570.

Engel, G. L. (1977). The need for a new medical model: a challenge for biomedicine. *Science*, *196*(4286), 129–136.

Erikson, E. H. (1968). *Identity: Youth and crisis.* New York, NY: Norton.

Erikson, E. H. (1982). *The life cycle completed: A review*. New York, NY: Norton.

Forbes, E. E., & Dahl, R. E. (2010). Pubertal development and behavior: Hormonal activation of social and motivational tendencies. *Brain and Cognition*, *72*(1), 66–72.

French, S., Seidman, E., Allen, L., & Aber, J. L. (2006). The development of ethnic identity during adolescence. *Developmental Psychology*, *42*(1), 1–10.

Fung, J., Guo, S., Jin, J., Bear, L., & Lau, A. (2016). A pilot randomized trial evaluating a School-Based Mindfulness Intervention for ethnic minority youth. *Mindfulness*, *7*(4), 819–828. DOI:10.1007/s12671-016-0519

Gitterman, A., & Germain, C. B. (2008). *The life model of social work practice: Advances in theory and practice*. New York, NY: Columbia University Press.

Helms, J. E. (Ed.). (1990). *Black and White racial identity: Theory, research and practice*. Westport, CT: Greenwood Press.

Helms, J. E. (2007). Some better practices for measuring racial and ethnic identity constructs. *Journal of Counseling Psychology*, *54*(3), 235–246.

Hinton, D. E., Pich, V., Hofmann, S. G., & Otto, M. W. (2013). Acceptance and mindfulness techniques as applied to refugee and ethnic minority populations with PTSD: Examples from "Culturally Adapted CBT." *Cognitive and Behavioral Practice*, *20*(1), 33–46.

Hofmann, W., Schmeichel, B. J., & Baddeley, A. D. (2012). Executive functions and self-regulation. *Trends in Cognitive Sciences*, *16*(3), 174–180.

Hollon, S. D., & Beck, A. T. (2004). Cognitive and cognitive-behavioral therapies. In M. J. Lambert (Ed.), *Bergin and Garfield's handbook of psychotherapy and behavior change* (5th ed.) (pp. 447–492). New York: John Wiley.

Hölzel, B. K., Carmody, J., Vangel, M., Congleton, C., Yerramsetti, S. M., Gard, T., & Lazar, S. W. (2011). Mindfulness practice leads to increases in regional brain gray matter density. *Psychiatry Research: Neuroimaging*, *191*(1), 36–43.

Hölzel, B. K., Lazar, S. W., Gard, T., Schuman-Olivier, Z., Vago, D. R., & Ott, U. (2011). How does mindfulness meditation work? Proposing mechanisms of action from a conceptual and neural perspective. *Perspectives on Psychological Science*, *6*(6), 537–559.

Jones, M. D., & Galliher, R. V. (2007). Ethnic identity and psychosocial functioning in Navajo adolescents. *Journal of Research on Adolescence*, *17*(4), 683–696.

Keefe, T. (1996). Meditation and social work treatment. In F. J. Turner (Ed.), *Social work treatment: Interlocking theoretical approaches* (2nd ed.) (pp. 434–460). New York, NY: The Free Press.

Kroger, J., Martinussen, M., & Marcia, J. E. (2010). Identity status change during adolescence and young adulthood: A meta-analysis. *Journal of Adolescence*, *33* (5), 683–698.

Larson, R. W. (2000). Toward a psychology of positive youth development. *American Psychologist*, *55*(1), 170.

Lazar, S. W., Bush, G., Gollub, R. L., Fricchione, G. L., Khalsa, G., & Benson, H. (2000). Functional brain mapping of the relaxation response and meditation. *Neuroreport, 11*(7), 1581–1585.

Lerner, R. M. (2004). *Liberty: Thriving and civic engagement among America's youth.* Thousand Oaks, CA: Sage.

Lerner, R. M., Lamb, M. E., & Freund, A. M. (2010). *The handbook of life-span development, social and emotional development* (Vol. 2). Hoboken, NJ: John Wiley.

Lerner, R. M., Lerner, J. V., Almerigi, J. B., Theokas, C., Phelps, E., Gestsdottir, S., & Smith, L. M. (2005). Positive Youth Development, Participation in community youth development programs, and community contributions of fifth-grade adolescent: Findings from the first wave of the 4-H study of Positive Youth Development. *The Journal of Early Adolescence, 25*(1), 17–71.

Luders, E., Kurth, F., Mayer, E. A., Toga, A. W., Narr, K. L., & Gaser, C. (2012). The unique brain anatomy of meditation practitioners: alterations in cortical gyrification. *Frontiers in Human Neuroscience, 6*(34), 1–9.

Lutz, A., Slagter, H. A., Dunne, J. D., & Davidson, R. J. (2008). Attention regulation and monitoring in meditation. *Trends in Cognitive Sciences, 12*(4), 163–169. DOI:10.1016/j.tics.2008.01.005

Marcia, J. E. (1966). Development and validation of ego identity status. *Journal of Personality and Social Psychology, 3*(5), 551–558.

Marcia, J. (1980). Identity in adolescence. In J. Adelson (Ed.), *Handbook of Adolescent Psychology* (pp. 159–187). New York, NY: John Wiley.

Marcia, J. E., Waterman, A. S., Matteson, D. R., Archer, S. L., & Orlofsky, J. L. (Eds.). (1993). *Ego identity: A handbook for psychosocial research.* New York, NY: Springer Verlag.

Meeus, W., Iedema, J., Helsen, M., & Vollebergh, W. (1999). Patterns of adolescent identity development: Review of literature and longitudinal analysis. *Developmental Review, 19*(4), 419–461.

Nash, J. D. & Newberg, A. B. (2013). *Toward a unifying taxonomy and definition for meditation.* Jefferson Myrna Brind Center of Integration Medicine Faculty Papers. Paper 11. http://jdc.jefferson.edu/jmbcimfp/11

Organista, K. C. (2007). Solving Latino psychosocial and health problems: Theory, research, and populations. Hoboken, NJ: John J. Wiley.

Payne, M. (2014). Modern Social Work Theory (4th ed.). Chicago, IL: Lyceum Books.

Pfeifer, J. H., & Blakemore, S. J. (2012). Adolescent social cognitive and affective neuroscience: Past, present, and future. *Social Cognitive and Affective Neuroscience, 7*(1), 1–10.

Phinney, J. S., & Ong, A. D. (2007). Conceptualization and measurement of ethnic identity: Current status and future directions. *Journal of Counseling Psychology, 54*(3), 271–281.

Posner, M. I., & Rothbart, M. K. (2007). Research on attention networks as a model for the Integration of psychological science. *Annual Review of Psychology*, *58*, 1–23.

Prochaska, J. O., & DiClemente, C. C. (1982). Transtheoretical therapy: Toward a more integrative model of change. *Psychotherapy: Theory, Research and Practice*, *19*(3), 276–288.

Prochaska, J. O., & Norcross, J. C. (2007). *Systems of psychotherapy: A transtheoretical analysis* (6th ed.). Belmont, CA: Thomson Brooks/Cole.

Prochaska, J. O., Redding, C. A. & Evers, K. E. (2008). The transtheoretical model and stages of change. In K. Glanz, B. K. Rimer, and K. Viswanath (Eds.). *Health behavior and health education: Theory, research, and practice* (4th ed.) (pp. 97–121). San Francisco, CA: John Wiley.

Prochaska, J. O., & Velicer, W. F. (1997). The transtheoretical model of health behavior change. *American Journal of Health Promotion*, *12*(1), 38–48.

Rosen, A. (2006). Destigmatizing day-to-day practices: What developed countries can learn from developing countries. *World Psychiatry*, *5*(1), 21–24.

Roth, J. L., & Brooks-Gunn, J. (2003). Youth development programs: Risk, prevention and policy. *Journal of Adolescent Health*, *32*(3), 170–182.

Rueda, M. R., Posner, M. I., & Rothbart, M. K. (2005). The development of executive attention: Contributions to the emergence of self-regulation. *Developmental Neuropsychology*, *28*(2), 573–594.

Sanger, K. L., & Dorjee, D. (2015). Mindfulness training for adolescents: A neurodevelopmental perspective on investigating modifications in attention and emotion regulation using event-related brain potentials. *Cognitive, Affective, & Behavioral Neuroscience*, *15*(3), 696–711.

Sedlmeier, P., Eberth, J., Schwarz, M., Zimmermann, D., Haarig, F., Jaeger, S., & Kunze, S. (2012). The psychological effects of meditation: A meta-analysis. *Psychological Bulletin*, *138*(6), 1139–1171.

Seligman, M. E. P., & Csikszentmihalyi, M. (2000). *Positive psychology: An introduction. American Psychologist*, *55*(1), 5–14.

Shapiro, S. L., Carlson, L. E., Astin, J. A., & Freedman, B. (2006). Mechanisms of mindfulness. *Journal of Clinical Psychology*, *62*(3), 373–386.

Shapiro, S. L., & Schwartz, G. E. (2000). The role of intention in self-regulation: Toward intentional systemic mindfulness. In M. Boekaerts, P. R. Pintrich, & M. Zeidner (Eds.), Handbook of self-regulation (pp. 253–273). San Diego, CA: Academic Press. http://dx.doi.org/10.1016/B978-012109890-2/50037-8

Sharp, J. E., Niemiec, R. M., & Lawrence, C. (2016). Using Mindfulness-Based Strengths Practices with gifted populations. *Gifted Education International.* DOI:10.1177/0261429416641009

Shear, J. (Ed.). (2006). *The experience of meditation: Experts introduce the major traditions.* St. Paul, MN: Paragon House.

Sowell, E. R., Trauner, D. A., Gamst, A., & Jernigan, T. L. (2002). Development of cortical and subcortical brain structures in childhood and adolescence: A structural MRI study. *Developmental Medicine & Child Neurology*, *44*(01), 4–16.

Steinberg, L. (2005). Cognitive and affective development in adolescence. *Trends in Cognitive Sciences*, *9*(2), 69–74.

Stephen, J., Fraser, E., & Marcia, J. E. (1992). Moratorium-achievement (Mama) cycles in lifespan identity development: Value orientations and reasoning system correlates. *Journal of Adolescence*, *15*(3), 283–300.

Stevens, M. R. (2008). *Erik H. Erikson: explorer of identity and the life cycle.* London: Palgrave Macmillan.

Taber-Thomas, B., & Perez-Edgar, K. (2015). Emerging Adulthood brain development. In J. J. Arnett (Ed.). *The Oxford handbook of Emerging Adulthood* (pp. 126–141). Oxford: Oxford University Press.

Tang, Y. Y., Lu, Q., Fan, M., Yang, Y., & Posner, M. I. (2012). Mechanisms of white matter changes induced by meditation. *Proceedings of the National Academy of Sciences*, *109*(26), 10570–10574.

Travis, F., Haaga, D. A., Hagelin, J., Tanner, M., Arenander, A., Nidich, S., & Schneider, R. H. (2010). A self-referential default brain state: Patterns of coherence, power, and eLORETA sources during eyes-closed rest and Transcendental Meditation practice. *Cognitive Processing*, *11*(1), 21–30.

Tudge, J. R., Mokrova, I., Hatfield, B. E., & Karnik, R. B. (2009). Uses and misuses of Bronfenbrenner's bioecological theory of human development. *Journal of Family Theory & Review*, *1*(4), 198–210.

Umana-Taylor, A. J., Vargas-Chanes, D., Garcia, C. D., & Gonzales-Backen, M. (2008). A longitudinal examination of Latino adolescents' ethnic identity, coping with discrimination, and self-esteem. *Journal of Early Adolescence*, *28* (1), 16–50. DOI:10.1177/0272431607308666

Vago, D. R., & Silbersweig, D. A. (2012). Self-awareness, self-regulation, and self-transcendence (S-ART): A framework for understanding the neurobiological mechanisms of mindfulness. *Frontiers in Human Neuroscience*, *6*(296), 1–30. DOI:10.3389/fnhum.2012.00296

Wallace, B. A., & Shapiro, S. L. (2006). Mental balance and well-being: Building bridges between Buddhism and Western psychology. *American Psychologist*, *61* (7), 690–701. DOI:10.1037/0003-066X.61.7.690

Wisner, B. L. (2013). Less stress, less drama, and experiencing monkey mind: Benefits and challenges of a school-based meditation program for adolescents. *School Social Work Journal*, *38*(1), 49–63.

Wisner, B. L. (2014). An exploratory study of mindfulness meditation for alternative School students: Perceived benefits for improving school climate and student functioning. *Mindfulness*, *5*(6), 626–638.

Wisner, B. L., & Norton, C. L. (2013). Capitalizing on behavioral and emotional strengths of alternative high school students through group counseling to promote mindfulness skills. *The Journal for Specialists in Group Work, 38*(3), 207–224.

World Health Organization (2016). Adolescent development. Retrieved from http://www.who.int/maternal_child_adolescent/topics/adolescence/dev/en/

Yeh, C. J., & Huang, K. (1996). The collectivistic nature of ethnic identity development among Asian-American college students. *Adolescence, 31*(123), 645.

CHAPTER 3

Benefits of Mindfulness and Meditation for Adolescents

Introduction

The benefits of mindfulness and meditation practices for adolescents are wide-ranging and encompass the major domains of adolescent development. The importance of understanding current views of adolescence, meditation, and mindfulness within relevant theoretical foundations and contexts was discussed in Chapter 2. As mindfulness and meditation programs for adolescents proliferate, using these foundations and contexts, as well as available research, supports development and delivery of these programs to help adolescents.

In addition to a strong theoretical foundation, research findings from qualitative and quantitative studies on mindfulness and meditation practices provide essential information about what these practices can do for adolescents and how the practices can be applied in various settings. Program development also is informed by the wisdom of practice experience. This is consistent with the current emphasis on evidence-based practice, but also recognizes that those who work with adolescents may have important information that complements the research evidence. Combining research plus practice wisdom informs research questions and methods to substantiate the effective and ethical use of practice interventions (Council on Social Work Education, 2008). In this integrative approach, program development includes meeting the unique needs of adolescents through integration of evidence-based practice and practice wisdom.

The research literature on mindfulness and meditation practices for adolescents was briefly discussed in Chapters 1 and 2, and will be explored

B.L. Wisner, *Mindfulness and Meditation for Adolescents*,
DOI 10.1057/978-1-349-95207-6_3

in more detail in this chapter using a bio-psycho-social-cultural framework. This evidence base is growing as shown by initial meta-analyses and systematic reviews conducted on this topic (Felver, Celis-de Hoyos, Tezanos, & Singh, 2016; Zenner, Herrnleben-Kurz, & Walach, 2014; Zoogman, Goldberg, Hoyt, & Miller, 2015). Thus, in this chapter, the biological and neuroscience research about mindfulness and meditation practices for adolescents will be explored including information about physiological benefits and neurological changes to the brain. The benefits related to emotional, cognitive, and behavioral self-regulation skills also will be presented. Other psychological benefits of meditation practices for adolescent populations will be explored including heightened self-esteem, self-awareness, and development of trust. Synthesis of the literature about the impact of practicing mindfulness and meditation on social relationships and related cultural benefits also are addressed.

Using the bio-psycho-social-cultural framework to provide more details about the benefits of mindfulness and meditation practices for adolescents is not without its challenges. Most of the studies in this area describe multiple benefits to adolescents with these benefits spanning more than one category (e.g., both biological and psychological benefits of a particular mindfulness and meditation practice). Therefore, some studies will be mentioned in a number of the categories when multiple outcomes are presented in the findings.

Benefits of Mindfulness and Meditation with Adolescents

Biological Benefits

As mentioned in Chapter 2, adolescence is marked by extensive physiological and neural development (Forbes & Dahl, 2010). Some physiological and neural factors can be modified through mindfulness and meditation practices for adolescents. Studies substantiating these changes will be reviewed in this section, and selected studies will be used to illustrate programs in subsequent chapters.

Cardiovascular Reactivity

Meditation programs have been used to address cardiovascular reactivity in adolescents in the US. In particular, Transcendental Meditation (TM) was found to be effective for prevention and treatment of cardiovascular disease in adolescents and adults (Barnes & Orme-Johnson, 2012). Dr. Vernon Barnes and his colleagues, under the auspices of the Georgia Prevention Institute of the Georgia Health Sciences University, have conducted a number of controlled studies on the physiological effects of meditation for cardiovascular reactivity for prehypertensive and normotensive adolescents in the US. For example, TM programs were effective in decreasing resting systolic blood pressure and cardiovascular reactivity in response to acute stress (Barnes, Treiber, & Davis, 2001), and for reducing daytime systolic and diastolic blood pressure for high school students (Barnes, Treiber, & Johnson, 2004).

Similarly, a school-based mindfulness meditation (MM) program for middle school students also was effective for decreasing ambulatory heart rate, and ambulatory systolic and diastolic blood pressure (Barnes, Davis, Murzynowski, & Treiber, 2004). In another school-based program, participants with high-normal systolic blood pressure showed decreased systolic blood pressure and heart rate during school, reduced systolic blood pressure at night, and decreased overnight urinary sodium excretion rate following participation in a mindful breathing meditation program (Barnes, Pendergrast, Harshfield, & Treiber, 2008).

Furthermore, reductions in systolic and diastolic blood pressure were found for African American adolescents who participated in a mindful breathing group program during summer camp (Gregoski, Barnes, Tingen, Harshfield, & Treiber, 2011). Likewise, African American high school students at risk of essential hypertension showed pretest-posttest reductions in 24-hour systolic ambulatory blood pressure following participation in a mindfulness-based breathing awareness meditation intervention (Wright, Gregoski, Tingen, Barnes, & Treiber, 2011). Similar improvements in physiological functioning also were mentioned by Felver et al., (2016) in their systematic review of studies of youth who participated in school-based MBIs.

Physical Health

Physiological benefits were noted for high school senior girls who participated in a mindfulness curriculum in a US private school. They reported decreased tiredness and aches and pains following participation in the program (Broderick & Metz, 2009). In addition, adolescents in an urban environment in the US who participated in a mindfulness-based stress reduction (MBSR) program in a hospital pediatric and adolescent outpatient clinic reported decreased general discomfort and improved physical health (e.g., increased physical activity and healthier eating) (Sibinga, Kerrigan, Stewart, Johnson, Magyari, & Ellen, 2011).

Although there are a limited number of studies of the biological benefits of mindfulness and meditation practices for adolescents, it is clear that these practices provide adolescents with skills that help them modify physiological responses. This is important given the developmental neuroscience perspective discussed in Chapter 2. Providing adolescents with a practice that helps them gain control over biological processes allows young people to improve physiological self-regulation and brings greater levels of health and wellness to their lives.

Psychological Benefits

In addition to physiological changes in adolescence, wide-ranging psychological changes are experienced by adolescents. These psychological changes involve development of skills in a number of areas including emotional self-regulation skills, cognitive functioning, including executive functioning, and behavioral regulation (Keating, Lerner, & Steinberg, 2004). These self-regulatory processes are important factors in the successful navigation of adolescence, and the practice of self-regulation for adolescents involves use of metacognitive abilities coupled with a personal belief in the capacity to be successful along with the ability to garner the resources necessary to succeed, particularly in academic endeavors (Cleary & Zimmerman, 2004; Zimmerman, 1995). Changes in self-concept and identity formation are also important developmental markers for adolescents (Keating, 2004). Given the importance of these developmental factors related to self-regulation skills, the research establishing the emotional, cognitive, and behavioral benefits of mindfulness and meditation practices for diverse psychological variables is presented.

Emotional Self-Regulation

Many of the studies reporting psychological outcomes in the research on mindfulness and meditation for adolescents involve regulation of emotions and consequent improvements in well-being. Studies have been conducted in educational, clinical, and community settings with mindfulness-based practices, TM, the Center for Mind-Body Medicine's (CMBM) group programs, and the relaxation response (RR). Some of these studies are briefly reviewed here and are addressed in more detail in subsequent chapters.

Affective Regulation and Well-Being

General improvements in affective regulation for students in school-based mindfulness skills programs have been reported. For example, in a school-based TM intervention in the US, students reported improved emotional self-control, patience, tolerance, and increased relaxation and energy (Rosaen & Benn, 2006).

Similarly, school-based mindfulness-based programs have shown promise for improving affective regulation and well-being. Middle school students participated in a school-based program in the US that incorporated elements of MBSR and Tai Chi (i.e., a mind-body exercise combining movement, breathing, and awareness of the internal and external environment). Students reported a greater sense of well-being, calmness, and peacefulness during the program (Wall, 2005). Similar findings were reported by Broderick and Metz (2009) who found increased feelings of calmness and relaxation in US high school senior girls following participation in a mindfulness curriculum. Similarly, emotional self-regulation was evidenced by an increased sense of well-being for students following school-based mindfulness interventions in the UK (Huppert & Johnson, 2010; Kuyken et al., 2013) and in Hong Kong (Lau & Hue, 2011). Increased well-being was also reported for incarcerated youth who practiced an MBI in the US (Himelstein, Hastings, Shapiro, & Heery, 2012a). Likewise, students showed fewer emotional regulation difficulties and an increase in emotional self-regulation in response to a mindfulness skills program in the US (Metz, Frank, Reibel, Cantrell, Sanders, & Broderick, 2013). In addition, students in a US alternative high school reported increased calmness, relaxation, and emotional coping following a mindfulness intervention (Wisner, 2014). In the same study, teacher ratings also showed significant increases in student affective strengths for this population (e.g., identifies own feelings and expresses affection for others) following the MM intervention (Wisner & Norton, 2013). In programs including mindfulness skills, delivered by teachers in school-based programs in Canada, there were significant increases in scores on self-report measures of optimism (Schonert-Reichl & Lawlor, 2010; Schonert-Reichl et al., 2015). Other studies showed that students in school-based mindfulness skills program reported an increase in happiness after participation in programs in the Netherlands (Bögels, Hoogstad, van Dun, De Shutter, & Restifo, 2008) and the US (Wisner & Starzec, 2016).

The systematic review of MBIs conducted by Felver et al. (2016) also supported these findings related to emotional regulation, affective regulation, and well-being. They reported improved positive affect and optimism, and a reduction in affective disturbances and suicidal ideation for youth who participated in school-based MBIs.

Emotional Intelligence and Emotional Arousal

Improvements in emotional intelligence have been reported for US adolescents participating in a school-based RR program (Benson et al., 1994) and in a school-based TM program (Rosaen & Benn, 2006). In addition, school-based mindfulness programs show promise for stimulating increases in emotional intelligence and changes in emotional arousal. For example, Mendelson, Greenberg, Dariotis, Gould, Rhoades, and Leaf (2010) reported that fourth and fifth graders in an urban public elementary school in the US showed lower emotional arousal scores when compared with the waitlist control group in a school-based mindfulness and yoga intervention.

Early adolescents in Canada who participated in a school-based curriculum with mindfulness exercises showed improvements in emotional control following participation in the program (Schonert-Reichl et al., 2015). Reductions in emotional problems were reported for adolescents participating in a mindfulness curriculum in a public school in Brazil (Waldemar, Rigatti, Menezes, Guimarães, Falceto, & Heldt, 2016). Similar findings occurred in other settings; for example, reductions in emotional discomfort occurred for adolescents who participated in an MBSR program in a US outpatient hospital setting (Sibinga et al., 2011).

Stress Management

The stress management benefits for adolescents in school-based settings are evident from several studies. Reductions in stress were reported for youth following a school-based TM program for US adolescents with attention deficit hyperactivity disorder (ADHD) (Grosswald, Stixrud, Travis, & Bateh, 2008). Decreases in perceived stress also were found for US high school students in a RR program combining meditation, mindfulness, imagery, and yoga with cognitive practices (Foret et al., 2012). Stress management benefits of school-based mindfulness programs also were evident in US programs (Bluth et al., 2016; Edwards, Adams, Waldo, Hadfield, & Biegel, 2014; Wisner, 2014; Wisner & Starzec, 2016) and in the UK (Kuyken et al., 2013). Interestingly, in a school-based yoga program for US middle school girls, the participants actually reported greater appraisal of stress when compared with the waitlist control group, but also showed increased coping (White, 2012).

Sibinga et al. (2011) also reported improvements in stress management for adolescents in an MBSR program in a hospital outpatient setting in the US. Similar findings were reported in a study that found reductions in perceived stress for incarcerated youth in the US who participated in an MBI group (Himelstein, Hastings, Shapiro, & Heery, 2012b). In addition, benefits of mindfulness training combined with cognitive-behavioral therapy (CBT) for youth incarcerated in an urban setting in the US included amelioration of the heightened stress typically experienced by youth incarcerated in a secure correctional facility (Leonard et al., 2013).

Anxiety, Depression, and PTSD

Participation in a mindfulness or meditation program often leads to improvements in emotional regulation. Increases in positive emotions may occur and enhanced regulation of challenging emotions is fostered after participation in these programs. For example, reductions in anxiety were found for participants of school-based mindfulness programs in the US (Beauchemin et al., 2008; Sibinga, Perry-Parrish, Cheung, Johnson, Smith, & Ellen, 2013), and in school-based TM programs in Taiwan (So & Orme-Johnson, 2001) and in the US (Grosswald et al., 2008).

Findings from several studies of school-based mindfulness programs indicated that students reported decreased depression or fewer depressive symptoms after participation in the programs. This was true for students in programs in the US (Beauchemin, Hutchins & Patterson, 2008; Bluth, Campo, Pruteanu-Malinici, Reams, Mullarkey, & Broderick, 2016; Edwards et al., 2014; Liehr & Diaz, 2010), in Hong Kong (Lau & Hue, 2011), in the UK (Kuyken et al., 2013), in Australia (Joyce, Etty-Leal, Zazryn, Hamilton, & Hassed, 2010), in a curriculum with mindfulness skills in Canada (Schonert-Reichl et al., 2015), and in a school-based group mindfulness program (adapted from mindfulness-based cognitive therapy and MBSR) in Belgium (Raes, Griffith, Van der Gucht, & Williams, 2014). Decreased anxiety also was found for US high school students in a RR program combining cognitive practices with meditation, mindfulness, imagery and yoga (Foret et al., 2012).

In clinical settings, MBIs were found to be helpful as one component of treatment for adolescents. For example, Bootzin and Stevens (2005) found reduced anxiety following the use of MBSR as one aspect of treatment for adolescents in a substance abuse treatment program in the US. Similarly, adolescent outpatients at a US psychiatric facility who received MBSR plus treatment-as-usual experienced reduced anxiety compared to controls (Biegel et al., 2009). Another study showed that, compared to a waitlist control group, children and early adolescents who participated in a mindfulness-based cognitive therapy (MBCT) group intervention program in an inner city university clinic in the US reported reduced anxiety (Semple, Lee, Dinelia, & Miller, 2010).

In addition, MBIs in clinical settings also were found to be helpful for reducing depression in adolescents. For example, reductions in depression were noted for adolescent outpatients at a US psychiatric facility who participated in MBSR plus treatment-as-usual (Biegel, Brown, Shapiro, & Schubert, 2009). Similar results were found for use of an MBI (adapted from MBCT) for adolescents at an academic center for clinical psychology in Belgium (Deplus, Billieux, Scharff, & Philippot, 2016) and for MBCT program participants in a mental health setting in England (Ames, Richardson, Payne, Smith, & Leigh, 2014). In another program based on mindfulness, cognitive-behavioral therapy, and mixed martial arts, reductions in anxiety were found in boys who participated in the program at a children's mental health center in Canada (Haydicky, Wiener, Badali, Milligan, & Ducharme, 2012).

Similar findings were reported in a community setting in which the CMBMs mind-body skills program for helping those in communities affected by trauma was used. Palestinian children and adolescents exposed to war in Gaza showed decreased hopelessness and depression and decreased post-traumatic stress disorder (PTSD) symptoms after participation in the program (Staples, Abdel Atti, & Gordon, 2011). Similarly, following participation in a school-based application of the CMBM group format model, Kosovar adolescents showed significant reductions in PTSD symptoms (Gordon, Staples, Blyta, & Bytyqi, 2004). In addition, in a second school-based study conducted with Kosovar adolescents, participants in the intervention group scored significantly lower on posttest PTSD symptom scores than did those in the waitlist control group (Gordon, Staples, Blyta, Bytyqi, & Wilson, 2008).

Anger

As stated, mindfulness and meditation programs also help adolescents regulate challenging emotions. This is illustrated by examples of emotional regulation of specific emotions, such as the management of anger. Adolescents may find new ways to manage anger following mindfulness and meditation programs. This was found in a program using TM interventions in the US (Grosswald et al., 2008; Rosaen & Benn, 2006) and in a mindfulness skills program in the US (Wisner & Starzec, 2016). This ability to observe the self and modify behaviors including anger is exemplified by the following "Adolescent Voices" quote by a teen boy who practiced mindfulness meditation.

Adolescent Voices

"It [meditation] just made me actually look about, it just made me think about like, oh wow,'cause after I stopped punching walls and everything, I was like, wow, I'm an angry kid when I get mad and, like, I don't like being angry."

Adolescent Mindfulness Meditation Practitioner
(Wisner & Starzec, 2016, p. 252)

In summary, these studies, along with the meta-analytic studies and systematic reviews (Felver et al., 2016; Zenner et al., 2014; Zoogman et al., 2015) show that there are a wide range of psychological benefits of mindfulness and meditation programs for adolescents. Meditation helps them reduce stress, regulate and manage emotions, and strengthen personal assets. Thus, healthy psychological functioning emerges from participation in mindfulness and meditation practices in a supportive environment. Theoretical perspectives that contribute to our understanding of these benefits for adolescents include the developmental neuroscience perspective and positive youth development (PYD).

Cognitive Self-Regulation

Cognitive development in adolescence includes advances in abstract thinking, reasoning, decision-making, executive functioning, and adolescent egocentrism (Keating, 2004; Piaget, 1969). Changes in consciousness and attentional capabilities also occur (Keating, 2004). This development can be supported by participation in mindfulness and meditation programs. Advances in cognitive functioning also may support social and emotional development. This is illustrated by the following "Adolescent Voices" quote from a student in a school-based mindfulness program.

Adolescent Voices

"Uh, [meditation] just made me think about life, especially when we did the walking meditation, just focusing and just thinking how life is good for me too."

Adolescent Mindfulness Meditation Practitioner
(Wisner & Starzec, 2016, p. 252)

Mindful Awareness and Mindfulness

Cognitive benefits, related to increased mindfulness, have been found in diverse school-based programs. For example, Bögels et al. (2008) reported that students in the Netherlands experienced enhancements in mindful awareness while performing a sustained attention test following school-based mindfulness training. Likewise, increased mindfulness was found for students in an English school who participated in a school-based mindfulness program (Huppert & Johnson, 2010), in an elementary school program incorporating mindfulness skills in Canada (Schonert-Reichl et al., 2015) and in a pilot study of a school-based mindfulness program in a US alternative high school (Bluth et al., 2016).

In addition, analysis of pretest-posttest data indicated that mindfulness scores increased following a school-based MBSR program for Latino middle school students in the rural US (Edwards et al., 2014). Similar findings also were reported for mindfulness programs in community and correctional settings. For example, mindfulness was increased for participants in an MBI for adolescents at an academic center for clinical psychology in Belgium (Deplus et al., 2016), and in an MBI for incarcerated adolescents in the US (Himelstein et al., 2012a).

Attention, Concentration, and Memory

Improvements in attention, concentration, and memory also occur for adolescents participating in mindfulness and meditation programs. For example, students reported that a school-based TM program in the US helped them improve concentration (Rosaen & Benn, 2006). In a related vein, public school students showed improvements in subsystems of attention including attentional alerting, conflict monitoring, and reactive control following a TM program in India (Baijal, Jha, Kiyonaga, Singh, & Srinivasan, 2011).

Self-reported declines in attention problems were reported for students engaging in a school-based mindfulness training in the Netherlands (Bögels et al., 2008). Alternative school students in a school-based MM program in the US reported improved ability to pay attention (Wisner, 2014). In a study also conducted in the US, working memory capacity was found to improve following a mindfulness intervention for public middle school students (Quach, Mano, & Alexander, 2016).

In addition, children and early adolescents who participated in an MBCT group intervention program in an inner city university clinic in the US showed fewer attention problems than those in the waitlisted control group (Semple et al., 2010). Similarly, improved performance on tests of attention following mindfulness training for adolescents in a community mental health setting in the Netherlands also was reported (Van de Weijer-Bergsma, Formsma, de Bruin & Bögels, 2012). Declines in attention problems also were found following an MBI for adolescents in a community mental health setting in the Netherlands (Van de Weijer-Bergsma et al., 2012). The benefits of mindfulness training combined with CBT for youth incarcerated in an urban setting in the US included less deterioration in attentional tasks when compared with a control group. In addition, for those in the MBI group who practiced mindfulness outside of the group session, performance degradation remained stable over time rather than showing enhanced degradation over time (Leonard et al., 2013).

Cognitive Control and Executive Functioning

Mindfulness and meditation programs for adolescents also help them control thinking. For example, Mendelson et al. (2010) found that US adolescents reported lower levels of rumination and intrusive thoughts following a school-based mindfulness and yoga intervention. In addition, Sibinga et al. (2013) reported that participants in a school-based MBSR group in the US showed less rumination than those in a comparison group (Sibinga et al., 2013). Likewise, in a school-based program integrating mindfulness, CBT, and mixed martial arts, participants showed improvements in secondary control (i.e., acceptance and positive thinking) and reductions in cognitive errors (e.g., catastrophizing) compared to the waitlist control group (Milligan et al., 2016).

Similarly, Schonert-Reichl et al. (2015) found that US adolescents improved in cognitive control following participation in a curriculum with mindfulness skills. In addition, cognitive benefits of a school-based mindfulness program for adolescents in the US included self-reported improvements in the ability to regulate thoughts and control thinking (e.g., decreased negative thoughts and increased beneficial thoughts) (Wisner & Starzec, 2016).

Participation in an MBI also was found to increase strategies for reducing repetitive unconstructive thoughts for adolescents in an academic center for clinical psychology in Belgium (Deplus et al., 2016).

Consistent with these findings were studies showing improvements in executive functioning for adolescents following participation in a community mental health center's mindfulness-based program in the Netherlands (Van de Weijer-Bergsma et al., 2012) and in the US following a school-based TM intervention for adolescents with ADHD (Grosswald et al., 2008).

Academic Performance and School Functioning

Not surprisingly, given the cognitive benefits of mindfulness and meditation programs, studies also showed self-reported improvement in academic performance for students in a TM program in the US (Rosaen & Benn, 2006) and improved academic performance (from teacher ratings) for adolescents with learning disabilities following an MM program in the US (Beauchemin et al., 2008). In addition, pretest-posttest teacher ratings showed student improvements in school functioning (e.g., pays attention in class and completes school tasks on time) for US alternative high school students who participated in an MM program (Wisner & Norton, 2013).

A multi-year study of the RR curriculum was conducted in a US middle school with primarily ethnic minority youth in an inner city environment. Higher grade point averages and work habit scores were noted for students following participation in the program and more exposure to the curriculum was related to greater improvement in academic scores (Benson et al., 2000). Furthermore, increases on measures of practical intelligence and creativity were found for adolescents in Taiwan following participation in school-based TM programs (in a series of three studies) (So & Orme-Johnson, 2001). In addition, a targeted TM program offered to at-risk public urban middle school students in the US was shown to result in greater improvements on both English and math scores compared to students in the control group (Nidich et al., 2011). Perceived improvements in school achievement also were noted for participants in an outpatient MBSR program in a clinic in the US (Sibinga et al., 2011).

In summary, adolescents participating in mindfulness and meditation programs may find themselves experiencing a wide range of cognitive benefits. Mindfulness and attention levels may increase and improvements in academic performance and school functioning are possible. These benefits are among those shown in the studies reviewed here and reported in the meta-analytic studies and reviews of mindfulness programs for adolescents (Felver et al. 2016; Zenner et al., 2014; Zoogman et al., 2015). These findings are consistent with the role that developmental neuroscience, the cognitive-behavioral perspective, and PYD play in explaining how these cognitive benefits arise. Fostering cognitive strengths is likely to facilitate emotional and behavioral self-regulation and thereby improve coping skills.

Behavioral Self-Regulation

As an adolescent matures, situations and contexts that challenge the ability to control behavior or responses to stressful situations may occur. Adolescents also may encounter difficulties with sleep behavior or may act aggressively when challenged. They may act in ways contrary to expectations of parents or school personnel. These behavioral self-regulation challenges may lead to heightened stress or punishments and reprimands. In contrast, successful behavioral self-regulation contributes to personal resiliency (Gardner, Dishion, & Connell, 2008). Mindfulness and meditation programs offer a strengths-based method to enhance resilience as an alternative to these challenges as evidenced by the following "Adolescent Voices" statement offered by an adolescent in a mindfulness-based school program.

Adolescent Voices

"Because, um, like in school I would get frustrated with some of the teachers, and then, I'd just sometimes ignore them, but yeah, I think it's a typical thing that most kids do. [Now,] well, I just listen to what they have to say and then I just calm down. I just go back to doing my work."

Adolescent Mindfulness Meditation Practitioner
(Wisner & Starzec, 2016, p. 254)

Sleep Behavior

Improvements in sleep behavior were reported for adolescents who participated in school-based mindfulness programs in the US. For example, this was true for middle school students who participated in a program with aspects of MBSR and Tai Chi (Wall, 2005), for alternative high school students in an MM program (Wisner & Starzec, 2016), and for adolescents in an MBSR program (Sibinga et al., 2011). In a clinical setting, Bootzin and Stevens (2005) reported improved sleep for US adolescents who had participated in a program including MBSR as one aspect of treatment for insomnia.

Behavior Problems

Changes in behavior problems also have been assessed in mindfulness and meditation studies with adolescents. For example, a school-based TM program in the US was found to help students make behavioral changes (Barnes, Bauza, & Treiber, 2003). Students who participated in the program showed fewer missed class periods, fewer rule violations, and fewer days suspended from school compared to the control group. Reductions in behavior problems also were shown following a school-based TM intervention for US adolescents with ADHD (Grosswald et al., 2008).

Joyce et al. (2010) reported similar self-reported declines in behavior problems following a school-based mindfulness intervention in Australia. In addition, general self-regulation skills increased in US adolescents participating in a school-based yoga program (White, 2012). Another study showed that teacher reports indicated a decrease in aggression for Canadian adolescents who participated in a school-based program including mindfulness skills (Schonert-Reichl et al., 2015).

Van de Weijer-Bergsma et al. (2012) showed self-reported declines in behavior problems in adolescents with ADHD following an MBI program in a community mental health setting in the Netherlands. Likewise, children and early adolescents participating in an MBCT intervention in an inner city university clinic in the US showed reductions in behavior problems compared to those in a waitlist control group (Semple et al., 2010). General self-regulation skills also increased in US adolescents participating in mindfulness programs in juvenile centers (Himelstein, Hastings, Shapiro, & Heery, 2012a, 2012b). In another program integrating mindfulness, CBT, and mixed martial arts, improvements in parent-rated externalizing behavior, oppositional defiant problems, and conduct problems were reported for boys who participated in the program at a children's mental health center in Canada (Haydicky et al., 2012).

Reductions in impulsivity were noted for adolescents who participated in a mindfulness-based substance abuse treatment program for incarcerated youth in the US (Himelstein, 2011) and for those who participated in an MBI program at an academic center for clinical psychology in Belgium (Deplus et al., 2016). Reductions in hostility also have been reported following a mindfulness-based breathing awareness intervention for African American high school students in the US (Wright et al., 2011) and for participants in an outpatient clinic

MBSR program for US adolescents (Sibinga et al., 2011). Improved human immunodeficiency virus (HIV) medication adherence for HIV-infected participants in this program was also noted (Sibinga et al., 2011).

Another MBI called *Meditation on the Soles of the Feet* combines acceptance of emotions and redirection of attention to the sensations in the soles of the feet. This practice has been used to help US adolescents diagnosed with a variety of conditions, including intellectual disabilities, conduct disorder, autism spectrum disorders, and behavioral problems. This technique was shown to reduce aggression in adolescents at risk of expulsion from school due to aggressive behaviors associated with conduct disorder (Singh et al., 2007). This same technique was shown to reduce physical aggression at home in adolescents diagnosed with autism spectrum disorders (Singh et al., 2011), and reduced verbal and physical aggression in students with Prader-Willi syndrome (Singh, Lancioni, Myers, Karazsia, Courtney, & Nugent, 2016).

In summary, the studies of behavioral self-regulation show that mindfulness and meditation practices and programs for adolescents can contribute to successful functioning through improved sleep behavior and reduced aggression, and improvements in school-related behavior. These findings also were supported by Felver et al. (2016) in their systematic review of school-based MBIs. This is consistent with developmental neuroscience, cognitive-behavioral theory, and PYD. School and clinic personnel can capitalize on brain development by introducing practices that help adolescents regulate thoughts and behaviors that may be ordinarily viewed as outside of their control. By showing adolescents that positive behavior changes in sleep and behavior regulation can be strengthened through application of mindfulness and meditation, the adolescent moves toward positive functioning consistent with PYD.

Intrapersonal Psychological Strengths

As adolescents mature, the psychological aspects of self-awareness, self-esteem, and ability to trust self and others contribute to optimal functioning. Offering an adolescent practices and interventions that promote these personal attributes helps them maximize their potential for success. Mindfulness and meditation programs can assist in these efforts as illustrated in the following "Adolescent Voices" quote by an adolescent mindfulness meditation practitioner.

Adolescent Voices

"We started meditation at 2 minutes and now we can breeze through it like it's nothing and I have noticed that when I do meditation I feel relaxed. I used to never close my eyes and now I can close my eyes. I used to trust only like four people. Now I trust just about everyone."

Adolescent Mindfulness Meditation Practitioner
(Wisner, 2014, p. 633)

Self-Awareness, Self-Esteem, and Trust

Several studies have shown that mindfulness and meditation programs for youth influence self-awareness, self-esteem, and trust. For example, increases in self-esteem and internal locus of control were found in response to a RR program for US high school students (Benson et al., 1994), and perceived increases in self-awareness were found for middle school students in the US participating in a program combining aspects of MBSR and Tai Chi (Wall, 2005), and for alternative high school students in an MM program in the US (Wisner & Starzec, 2016). Also, an increase in self-acceptance was noted for students following participation in a school-based mindfulness curriculum in the US (Broderick & Metz, 2009).

Increases in self-esteem were found for US students in a TM program (Rosaen & Benn, 2006) and for participants in a school-based yoga program in the US (White, 2012). Self-compassion scores increased following a school-based MBSR program for Latino middle school students in the US (Edwards et al., 2014). In addition, a school-based program integrating mindfulness in English schools showed that participants exhibited increased ego-resilience after participation in the program (Huppert & Johnson, 2010). Adolescents also reported learning to trust through participation in a school-based MM program in the US (Wisner & Starzec, 2016). In other settings, increases in self-esteem also were found for US adolescent psychiatric outpatients following an MBSR plus treatment-as-usual program (Biegel et al., 2009).

As mentioned, optimal functioning is supported by a strong sense of self and connection with others. However, it is not uncommon for adolescents to experience periods of self-doubt and self-consciousness. These experiences may be exacerbated by stressful circumstances and unpredictable social relationships. Time spent in meditation and mindfulness may provide a time for self-exploration and self-examination leading to more comfort with self and others. In addition, interrupting uncomfortable thoughts and emotions makes room for positive thoughts and feelings resulting in deeper levels of self-awareness, higher self-esteem, and more trust in self and others. Through these mindfulness and meditation practices, adolescents may explore their motivations, desires, and fears without being overwhelmed. These psychological factors play a pivotal role in healthy functioning in the contexts of developmental neuroscience, cognitive-behavioral theory, adolescent identity development, PYD, and the systems perspective.

While developmental neuroscience and cognitive-behavioral theory contribute to understanding advances in intrapersonal strengths, the primary factors promoting these strengths may be related to adolescent identity development, the systems perspective, and PYD. In this circular process adolescents develop a sense of who they are as they engage in self-awareness and grow in self-esteem. This then fosters trust in self and others as an adolescent interacts with others in various systems. If an adolescent is exposed to opportunities that promote this type of growth and self-discovery with an emphasis on self-acceptance and identity exploration, positive relationships with others are fostered. Thus, the success of social relationships also depends on these intrapersonal factors as demonstrated in the next section.

Social Benefits

Moving from childhood to adolescence involves changes in family and social relationships with an emphasis on more autonomy from parents and strengthening relationships with peers. This transition may progress smoothly, resulting in maintaining strong and supportive family and peer relationships or may be marked by challenges in these relationships. When challenges occur, mindfulness and meditation programs have the potential to strengthen relationships and reduce conflict.

Strengthening Relationships

Adolescent participants in mindfulness and meditation programs are likely to build positive relationships with peers, family members, and teachers. For example, these findings were supported with qualitative data from students in a US alternative high school (Wisner, 2014; Wisner & Starzec, 2016) and with pretest-posttest teacher ratings showing student improvements in interpersonal strengths and family involvement (Wisner & Norton, 2013). Social connectedness also was increased for high school students in a US alternative school following program participation (Bluth et al., 2016).

In addition, teacher reports indicated improvements in social competence and empathy for Canadian students following participation in a curriculum with mindfulness skills (Schonert-Reichl et al., 2015). Likewise, participants increased in peer acceptance and were rated by peers as more prosocial compared to the control group (Schonert-Reichl et al., 2015). Similarly, self-reported improvements in prosocial behavior were reported for adolescents participating in a curriculum including mindfulness in a Brazilian public school (Waldemar et al., 2016). In another program at a children's mental health center in Canada, improvement on parent-rated social problems was reported for boys who participated in a program integrating mindfulness, CBT, and mixed martial arts (Haydicky et al., 2012).

Reducing Conflict

Sibinga et al. (2011) found that adolescents in an MBSR program in an outpatient clinic in the US reported perceived improvements in interpersonal relationships and reported less conflict in these relationships. Although few studies address changes at the school community level, analysis of quantitative and qualitative data collected from students in a US alternative high school indicated that students found MM to lead to a more positive school atmosphere (Wisner, 2014). In fact, these students judged the systemic effects of meditation to be among the most important changes that occurred from an 8-week course of MM offered in the school setting.

Thus, in addition to findings from the Felver et al. (2016) systematic review of studies of youth who participated in school-based MBIs, this literature shows that engaging in mindfulness and meditation practices offers a means to monitor behavior affecting social relationships. These factors are consistent with the cognitive-behavioral theory, the systems perspectives, and PYD. As mindfulness and meditation practices help adolescents assess their thoughts and behaviors, they are in a position to reflect on how their behavior affects others. Positive practices, including mindfulness and meditation practices, offer opportunities for adolescents to repair relationships and promote efforts toward building relationships. This is evidenced by the following "Adolescent Voices" quote.

Adolescent Voices

"I said some stuff on my home school bus [about another student] and she heard me say it about her and then I didn't think it was so mean, but then... I sat down with you guys and I was meditating. And then I came out of it and then I was apologizing to her'cause I felt bad after I thought about what I had said and everything."

Adolescent Mindfulness Meditation Practitioner
(Wisner & Starzec, 2016, p. 253)

Cultural Benefits

Cultural factors include elements related to spiritualty, religion, ethnicity, and language. While mindfulness and meditation are often used for spiritual and religious purposes, in secular settings, the mind-body perspective with an emphasis on health and well-being is more likely to be employed. However, it makes sense to address these aspects of development to maintain the holistic approach of the bio-psycho-social-cultural perspective used in this book.

Spirituality is an important developmental factor for many adolescents and adolescents may be open to spiritual exploration (Good & Willoughby, 2008). In addition, spirituality and religion often serve as protective factors for adolescents (Cotton, Zebracki, Rosenthal, Tsevat, & Drotar, 2006). Adolescents, depending on their spiritual and religious affiliations, may seek the cultural aspects of mindfulness and meditation experiences. One example of supporting young people with a mindfulness practice from a religious underpinning is Mindfulkids (https://mindfulkids.wordpress.com/about/). This site is affiliated with the international Zen meditation center, Plum Village, in France.

Spiritual Factors

Delivery of mindfulness and acceptance-based practices and programs is supported by understanding an individual within relevant cultural contexts (Hwang, 2011). This is illustrated in the research with adolescents. For example, in an evaluation of yoga and meditation training with adolescent sex offenders in the US, it was found that spiritual factors were important for some of the participants (Derezotes, 2000). In addition, US middle school students mentioned a sense of connection with nature in response to a combined MBSR and Tai Chi program (Wall, 2005). In other research, those who participated in a spirituality development class for urban homeless youth in the US showed posttest improvement on self-report measures of spirituality, mental wellness, psychological symptoms, and resilience (Grabbe, Nguy, & Higgins, 2012). Spiritual growth in girls also was noted following participation in a RR intervention (Foret et al., 2012). The potential for meditation to help adolescents explore these factors is illustrated in the following "Adolescent Voices" quote.

Adolescent Voices

"Meditation allows the students to think about ourselves, think about who we are."

Adolescent Mindfulness Meditation Practitioner
(Wisner, 2014, p. 633)

Ethnicity

The importance of ethnicity also has been addressed in mindfulness programs adapted to meet the unique needs of ethnic minority and immigrant populations (Hinton, Pich, Hofmann, & Otto, 2013). For example, meditation programs have been conducted to address cardiovascular concerns in African American adolescents (Barnes et al., 2008; Barnes, Treiber, & Johnson, 2004; Gregoski et al., 2011; Wright et al., 2011) and TM has the potential to reduce psychological distress in racial and ethnic minority students (Elder et al., 2011).

It is evident from the findings of these studies that, although cultural factors are not generally the focus of secular mindfulness and meditation programs for adolescents, they do offer a potentially important resource for youth. These factors are consistent with PYD and may be explored with adolescents in secular contexts in a culturally sensitive manner (with parental permission).

Summary

The mindfulness and meditation literature about practices and programs for adolescents has expanded quickly. This overview of the literature shows the evolution from a few qualitative and quasi-experimental studies to a number of randomized studies, research reviews, and meta-analyses. These efforts, placed in a theoretical context with an understanding of the practice wisdom of those who have worked directly with adolescents offers a good foundation for moving forward as mindfulness and meditation practices and programs for adolescents become more prevalent in schools, clinics, and community settings. This chapter provides a strong rationale for using mindfulness and meditation with adolescents. The benefits, as evidenced by the broad range of studies presented here, include biological, psychological, social, and self-regulation benefits. In addition, mindfulness and meditation practices and programs lead to increased self-awareness, self-esteem, and trust in self and others. Cultural benefits also may be identified that contribute to spiritual development.

Meditation offers adolescents the opportunity to learn how to observe their reactions and to modify these reactions. This increases emotional flexibility and contributes to increases in positive emotions and reductions in negative emotions. Similarly, adolescents may become overtaken by their emotions and an ongoing practice of meditation can help to circumvent the dominance of emotions and the ruminating thoughts that may occur. Episodes of anger, sadness, and anxiety are not uncommon in adolescents, and the simple emotional and behavioral regulation skills of meditation offer opportunities for coping with these feelings in a positive way. Learning to tolerate frustrating circumstances while increasing behavioral self-control and improving emotional regulation occur with extended meditation practice. In subsequent chapters, this research is explored in more depth in the context of programming in educational, clinical, home, community, and residential settings.

References

Ames, C. S., Richardson, J., Payne, S., Smith, P., & Leigh, E. (2014). Mindfulness-based cognitive therapy for depression in adolescents. *Child and Adolescent Mental Health*, *19*(1), 74–78. DOI:10.1111/camh.12034

Baijal, S., Jha, A., Kiyonaga, A., Singh, R., & Srinivasan, N. (2011). The influence of concentrative meditation training on the development of attention networks during early adolescence. *Frontiers in Psychology*, *2*(153), 1–9.

Barnes, V. A., & Orme-Johnson, D. W. (2012). Prevention and treatment of cardiovascular disease in adolescents and adults through the Transcendental Meditation® program: A research review update. *Current Hypertension Reviews*, *8*(3), 227–242.

Barnes, V. A., Treiber, F. A., & Davis, H. C. (2001). Impact of Transcendental Meditation on cardiovascular function at rest and during acute stress in adolescents with normal blood pressure. *Journal of Psychosomatic Research*, *51*(4), 597–605.

Barnes, V. A., Bauza, L. B., & Treiber, F. A. (2003). Impact of stress reduction on negative school behavior in adolescents. *Health and Quality of Life Outcome, 1* (10). DOI:10.1186/1477-7525-1-10

Barnes, V. A., Davis, H. C., Murzynowski, J. B., & Treiber, F. A. (2004). Impact of meditation on resting and ambulatory blood pressure and heart rate in youth. *Psychosomatic Medicine, 66*(6), 909–914.

Barnes, V. A., Treiber, F. A., & Johnson, M. H. (2004). Impact of Transcendental Meditation on ambulatory blood pressure in African American adolescents. *American Journal of Hypertension, 17*(4), 366–369.

Barnes, V. A., Pendergrast, R. A., Harshfield, G. A., & Treiber, F. A. (2008). Impact of breathing awareness meditation on ambulatory blood pressure and sodium handling in prehypertensive African American adolescents. *Ethnicity & Disease, 18*(1), 1–5.

Beauchemin, J., Hutchins, T. L., & Patterson, F. (2008). Mindfulness meditation may lessen anxiety, promote social skills, and improve academic performance among adolescents with learning disabilities. *Complementary Health Practice Review, 13*(1), 34–45.

Benson, H., Kornhaber, A., Kornhaber, C., LeChanu, M. N., Zuttermeister, P. C., Myers, P., & Friedman, R. (1994). Increases in positive psychological characteristics with a new relaxation-response curriculum in high school students. *Journal of Research and Development in Education, 27*(4), 226–231.

Benson, H., Wilcher, M., Greenberg, B., Higgins, E., Ennis, M., Zuttermeister, P. C., & Friedman, R. (2000). Academic performance among middle-school students after exposure to a relaxation response curriculum. *Journal of Research and Development in Education, 33*(3), 156–165.

Biegel, G. M, Brown, K. W., Shapiro, S. L, & Schubert, C. (2009). Mindfulness-based stress reduction for the treatment of adolescent psychiatric outpatients: A randomized clinical trial. *Journal of Clinical and Consulting Psychology, 77*(5), 855–866.

Bluth, K., Campo, R. A., Pruteanu-Malinici, S., Reams, A., Mullarkey, M., & Broderick, P. C. (2016). A school-based mindfulness pilot study for ethnically diverse at-risk adolescents. *Mindfulness, 7*(1), 90–104. DOI:10.1007/s12671-014-0376-1

Bögels, S., Hoogstad, B., Van Dun, L., De Shutter, S., & Restifo, K. (2008). Mindfulness training for adolescents with externalising disorders and their parents. *Behavioural and Cognitive Psychotherapy, 36*, 193–209.

Bootzin, R. R., & Stevens, S. J. (2005). Adolescents, substance abuse, and the treatment of insomnia and daytime sleepiness. *Clinical Psychology Review, 25* (5), 629–644.

Broderick, P. C., & Metz, S. (2009). Learning to BREATHE: A pilot trial of a mindfulness curriculum for adolescents. *Advances in School Mental Health Promotion 2*(1), 35–46.

Cleary, T. J., & Zimmerman, B. J. (2004). Self-regulation empowerment program: A school-based program to enhance self-regulated and self-motivated cycles of student learning. *Psychology in the Schools, 41*(5), 537–550.

Cotton, S., Zebracki, K., Rosenthal, S. L., Tsevat, J., & Drotar, D. (2006). Religion/spirituality and adolescent health outcomes: A review. *Journal of Adolescent Health, 38*(4), 472–480.

Council on Social Work Education. (2008). *Educational policy and accreditation standards.* Retrieved from www.cswe.org/File.aspx?id=41861

Deplus, S., Billieux, J., Scharff, C., & Philippot, P. (2016). A mindfulness-based group intervention for enhancing self-regulation of emotion in late childhood and adolescence: A pilot study. *International Journal of Mental Health and Addiction, 14*(5), 775–790.

Derezotes, D. (2000). Evaluation of yoga and meditation trainings with adolescent sex offenders. *Child and Adolescent Social Work Journal, 17*(2), 97–113.

Edwards, M., Adams, E. M., Waldo, M., Hadfield, O. D., & Biegel, G. M. (2014). Effects of a mindfulness group on Latino adolescent students: Examining levels of perceived stress, mindfulness, self-compassion, and psychological symptoms. *The Journal for Specialists in Group Work, 39*(2), 145–163.

Elder, C., Nidich, S., Colbert, R., Hagelin, J., Grayshield, L., Oviedo-Lim, D., . . . & Gerace, D. (2011). Reduced psychological distress in racial and ethnic minority students practicing the transcendental meditation program. *Journal of Instructional Psychology, 38*(2), 109–117.

Felver, J. C., Celis-De Hoyos, C. E., Tezanos, K., & Singh, N. N. (2016). A systematic review of mindfulness-based interventions for youth in school settings. *Mindfulness, 7*(1), 34–45.

Forbes, E. E., & Dahl, R. E. (2010). Pubertal development and behavior: Hormonal activation of social and motivational tendencies. *Brain and Cognition, 72*(1), 66–72.

Foret, M. M., Scult, M., Wilcher, M., Chudnofsky, R., Malloy, L., Hasheminejad, N., & Park, E. R. (2012). Integrating a relaxation response-based curriculum into a public high school in Massachusetts. *Journal of Adolescence, 35*(2), 325–332.

Gardner, T. W., Dishion, T. J., & Connell, A. M. (2008). Adolescent self-regulation as resilience: Resistance to antisocial behavior within the deviant peer context. *Journal of Abnormal Child Psychology, 36*(2), 273–284.

Good, M., & Willoughby, T. (2008). Adolescence as a sensitive period for spiritual development. *Child Development Perspectives, 2*(1), 32–37.

Gordon, J. S., Staples, J. K., Blyta, A., & Bytyqi, M. (2004). Treatment of Posttraumatic Stress Disorder in postwar Kosovo high school students using mind-body skills groups: A pilot study. *Journal of Traumatic Stress, 17*(2), 143–147.

Gordon, J. S., Staples, J. K., Blyta, A., Bytyqi, M., & Wilson, A. T. (2008). Treatment of posttraumatic stress disorder in postwar Kosovar adolescents using mind-body skills groups: A randomized controlled trial. *The Journal of Clinical Psychiatry*, 69(9), 1469–1476.

Grabbe, L., Nguy, S. T., & Higgins, M. K. (2012). Spirituality development for homeless youth: A mindfulness meditation feasibility pilot. *Journal of Child and Family Studies*, *21*(6), 925–937.

Gregoski, M.J., Barnes, V.A., Tingen, M.S., Harshfield, G.A., & Treiber, F. A. (2011). Breathing awareness meditation and LifeSkills Training programs influence upon ambulatory blood pressure and sodium excretion among African American adolescents. *Journal of Adolescent Health*, *48*, 59–64.

Grosswald, S. J., Stixrud, W. R., Travis, F., & Bateh, M. A. (2008). Use of the transcendental meditation technique to reduce symptoms of attention deficit hyperactivity disorder (ADHD) by reducing stress and anxiety: An exploratory study. *Current Issues in Education*, *10(2)*. Retrieved from: http://cie.asu.edu/ojs/index.php/cieatasu/article/view/1569

Haydicky, J., Wiener, J., Badali, P., Milligan, K., & Ducharme, J. M. (2012). Evaluation of a mindfulness-based intervention for adolescents with learning disabilities and co-occurring ADHD and anxiety. *Mindfulness*, *3*(2), 151–164.

Himelstein, S. (2011). Mindfulness-based substance abuse treatment for incarcerated youth: A mixed method pilot study. *International Journal of Transpersonal Studies*, 30(1–2), 1–10.

Himelstein, S., Hastings, A., Shapiro, S., & Heery, M. (2012a). A qualitative investigation of the experience of a mindfulness-based intervention with incarcerated adolescents. *Child and Adolescent Mental Health*, *17*(4), 231–237.

Himelstein, S., Hastings, A., Shapiro, S., & Heery, M. (2012b). Mindfulness training for self-regulation and stress with incarcerated youth: A pilot study. *Probation Journal*, *59*(2), 151–165.

Hinton, D. E., Pich, V., Hofmann, S. G., & Otto, M. W. (2013). Acceptance and mindfulness techniques as applied to refugee and ethnic minority populations with PTSD: Examples from" Culturally Adapted CBT." *Cognitive and Behavioral Practice*, *20*(1), 33–46.

Huppert, F.A. & Johnson, D. M. (2010) A controlled trial of mindfulness training in schools: The importance of practice for an impact on well-being. *The Journal of Positive Psychology*, *5*(4), 264–274.

Hwang, W. C. (2011). Cultural adaptations: A complex interplay between clinical and cultural issues. *Clinical Psychology: Science and Practice*, *18*(3), 238–241.

Joyce, A., Etty-Leal, J., Zazryn, T., Hamilton, A., & Hassed, C. (2010). Exploring a mindfulness meditation program on the mental health of upper primary children: A pilot study. *Advances in School Mental Health Promotion*, *3*(2), 17–25.

Keating, D. P. (2004). Cognitive and brain development. In D. P. Keating, R. M. Lerner, and L. Steinberg (Eds.), *Handbook of Adolescent Psychology* (2nd ed.) (pp. 45–84). Hoboken, NJ: John Wiley.

Keating, D. P., Lerner, R. M., & Steinberg, L. (2004) (Eds.). *Handbook of Adolescent Psychology*. Hoboken, NJ: John Wiley.

Kuyken, W., Weare, K., Ukoumunne, O. C., Vicary, R., Motton, N., Burnett, R., & Huppert, F. (2013). Effectiveness of the mindfulness in schools programme: Non-randomised controlled feasibility study. *The British Journal of Psychiatry, 203*(2), 126–131.

Lau, N. S., & Hue, M. T. (2011). Preliminary outcomes of a mindfulness-based programme for Hong Kong adolescents in schools: Well-being, stress and depressive symptoms. *International Journal of Children's Spirituality, 16*(4), 315–330.

Leonard, N. R., Jha, A. P., Casarjian, B., Goolsarran, M., Garcia, C., Cleland, C. M., & Massey, Z. (2013). Mindfulness training improves attentional task performance in incarcerated youth: A group randomized controlled intervention trial. *Frontiers in Psychology, 4*, 792. DOI:10.3389/fpsyg.2013.00792

Liehr, P., & Diaz, N. (2010). A pilot study examining the effect of mindfulness on depression and anxiety for minority children. *Archives of Psychiatric Nursing, 24*(1), 69–71.

Mendelson, T., Greenberg, M. T., Dariotis, J. K., Gould, L. F., Rhoades, B. L., & Leaf, P. J. (2010). Feasibility and preliminary outcomes of a school-based mindfulness intervention for urban youth. *Journal of Abnormal Child Psychology, 38*(7), 985–994.

Metz, S. M., Frank, J. L., Reibel, D., Cantrell, T., Sanders, R., & Broderick, P. C. (2013). The effectiveness of the learning to BREATHE program on adolescent emotion regulation. *Research in Human Development, 10*(3), 252–272.

Milligan, K., Irwin, A., Wolfe-Miscio, M., Hamilton, L., Mintz, L., Cox, M., & Phillips, M. (2016). Mindfulness Enhances Use of Secondary Control Strategies in High School Students at Risk for Mental Health Challenges. *Mindfulness, 7*(1), 219–227.

Nidich, S., Mjasiri, S., Nidich, R., Rainforth, M., Grant, J., Valosek, L., & Zigler, R. (2011). Academic achievement and transcendental meditation: A study with at-risk urban middle school students. *Education, 131*(3), 556–564.

Piaget, J. (1969). The intellectual development of the adolescent. In G. Caplan & S. Lebovici (Eds.), *Adolescence: Psychosocial perspective* (pp. 22–26). New York, NY: Basic Books.

Quach, D., Mano, K. E. J., & Alexander, K. (2016). A randomized controlled trial examining the effect of mindfulness meditation on working memory capacity in adolescents. *Journal of Adolescent Health, 58*(5), 489–496.

Raes, F., Griffith, J. W., Van Der Gucht, K., & Williams, J. M. G. (2014). School-based prevention and reduction of depression in adolescents: A cluster-randomized controlled trial of a mindfulness group program. *Mindfulness, 5*(5), 477–486.

Rosaen, C. & Benn, R. (2006). The experience of Transcendental Meditation in middle school students: A qualitative report. *Explore, 2*(5), 422–425.

Schonert-Reichl, K. A., & Lawlor, M. S. (2010). The effects of a mindfulness-based education program on pre- and early adolescents' well-being and social and emotional competence. *Mindfulness, 1*(3), 137–151.

Schonert-Reichl, K. A., Oberle, E., Lawlor, M. S., Abbott, D., Thomson, K., Oberlander, T. F., & Diamond, A. (2015). Enhancing cognitive and social–emotional development through a simple-to-administer mindfulness-based school program for elementary school children: A randomized controlled trial. *Developmental Psychology, 51*(1), 52.

Semple, R., Lee, J., Dinelia, R., & Miller, L. (2010) A randomized trial of Mindfulness-Based Cognitive Therapy for children: Promoting mindful attention to enhance social-emotional resiliency in children. *Journal of Child and Family Studies, 19*(2), 218–229.

Sibinga, E. M., Kerrigan, D., Stewart, M., Johnson, K., Magyari, T., & Ellen, J. M. (2011). Mindfulness-based stress reduction for urban youth. *The Journal of Alternative and Complementary Medicine, 17*(3), 213–218.

Sibinga, E. M. S., Perry-Parrish, C., Cheung, S., Johnson, S. B., Smith, M., & Ellen, J. M. (2013). School-based mindfulness instruction for urban male youth. A small randomized controlled trial. *Preventative Medicine, 57*(6), 799–801. DOI:10.1016/j.ypmed.2013.08.027

Singh, N. N., Lancioni, G. E., Joy, S. D. S., Winton, A. S. W., Sabaawi, M., Wahler, R. G., ... Singh, J. (2007). Adolescents with conduct disorder can be mindful of their aggressive behavior. *Journal of Emotional and Behavioral Disorders*, 15(1), 56–63. DOI:10.1177/10634266070150010601

Singh, N. N., Lancioni, G. E., Manikam, R., Winton, A. S. W., Singh, A. N. A., Singh, J.,... Singh, A. D. A. (2011). A mindfulness-based strategy for self-management of aggressive behavior in adolescents with autism. *Research in Autism Spectrum Disorders, 5*, 1153–1158. DOI:10.1016/j.rasd.2010.12.012

Singh, N. N., Lancioni, G. E., Myers, R. E., Karazsia, B. T., Courtney, T. M., & Nugent, K. (2016). A mindfulness-based intervention for selfmanagement of verbal and physical aggression by adolescents with Prader–Willi syndrome. *Developmental Neurorehabilitation*, 1–8. http://dx.doi.org/10.3109/17518423.2016.1141436

So, K., & Orme-Johnson, D. (2001). Three randomized experiments on the longitudinal effects of the Transcendental Meditation technique on cognition. *Intelligence, 29*, 419–440.

Staples, J. K., Abdel Atti, J. A., & Gordon, J. S. (2011). Mind-body skills groups for posttraumatic stress disorder and depression symptoms in Palestinian children and adolescents in Gaza. *International Journal of Stress Management, 18* (3), 246–262.

Van De Weijer-Bergsma, E., Formsma, A. R., De Bruin, E. I., & Bögels, S. M. (2012). The effectiveness of mindfulness training on behavioral problems and attentional functioning in adolescents with ADHD. *Journal of Child and Family Studies*, *21*(5), 775–787.

Waldemar, J. O. C., Rigatti, R., Menezes, C. B., Guimarães, G., Falceto, O., & Heldt, E. (2016). Impact of a combined mindfulness and social-emotional learning program on fifth graders in a Brazilian public school setting. *Psychology & Neuroscience*, *9*(1), 79–90.

Wall, R. B. (2005). Tai Chi and mindfulness based stress reduction in a Boston public middle school. *Journal of Pediatric Health Care*, *19*(4), 230–237.

White, L. S. (2012). Reducing stress in school-age girls through mindful yoga. *Journal of Pediatric Health Care*, *26*(1), 45–56. DOI:10.1016/j.pedhc.2011.01.002

Wisner, B. L. (2014). An exploratory study of mindfulness meditation for alternative school students: perceived benefits for improving school climate and student functioning. *Mindfulness*, *5*(6), 626–638.

Wisner, B. L., & Norton, C. L. (2013). Capitalizing on behavioral and emotional strengths of alternative high school students through group counseling to promote mindfulness skills. *The Journal for Specialists in Group Work*, *38*(3), 207–224.

Wisner, B. L., & Starzec, J. J. (2016). The process of personal transformation for adolescents practicing mindfulness skills in an alternative school setting. *Child and Adolescent Social Work Journal*, *33*(3), 245–257.

Wright, L. B., Gregoski, M. J., Tingen, M. S., Barnes, V. A., & Treiber, F. A. (2011). Impact of stress reduction interventions on hostility and ambulatory systolic blood pressure in African American adolescents. *Journal of Black Psychology* *37*(2): 210–233.

Zenner, C., Herrnleben-Kurz, S., & Walach, H. (2014). Mindfulness-based interventions in Schools: A systematic review and meta-analysis. *Frontiers in Psychology*, *5*(603), 1–20. http://dx.doi.org/10.3389/fpsyg.2014.00603

Zimmerman, B. J. (1995). Self-regulation involves more than metacognition: A social cognitive perspective. *Educational Psychologist*, *30*(4), 217–221.

Zoogman, S., Goldberg, S. B., Hoyt, W. T., & Miller, L. (2015). Mindfulness interventions with youth: A meta-analysis. *Mindfulness*, *6*(2), 290–302.

CHAPTER 4

Mindfulness and Meditation for Adolescents in Educational Settings

Introduction

The literature about mindfulness and meditation with adolescent populations has quickly expanded with new studies being published on a regular basis. Many of these studies take place in school-based settings. These settings include public schools, alternative schools, and private schools. In these settings, mindfulness and meditation programs may be offered in a universal manner (i.e., essentially provided to all students in the school), in a targeted manner (i.e., offering group interventions to students who have been identified as needing assistance), or in an intensive manner (i.e., offering individual intervention to students at a high level of need) (Felver, Doerner, Jones, Kaye, & Merrell, 2013). A comprehensive synthesis of this literature is included in Chapter 3, and this chapter offers examples of selected studies that establish the efficacy of school-based mindfulness and meditation programs and interventions using the universal, targeted, and intensive categorizations.

School-Based Mindfulness and Meditation Programs

School-Based Mindfulness Programs

Imagine a teacher in a classroom full of students. Some students are attending to the lesson plan. Others are talking with fellow classmates. Some students are looking out the window; others are sleepy and

B.L. Wisner, *Mindfulness and Meditation for Adolescents*,
DOI 10.1057/978-1-349-95207-6_4

disengaged. Some are even misbehaving and ignoring the teacher's directions. Now, imagine the teacher and the classroom three months later. You observe the teacher leading a brief mindfulness exercise at the beginning of class. Students become quiet and close their eyes. They take a few deep breaths and meditate for a few minutes. As the mindfulness exercise ends, the students are focused, attentive, and engaged in the lesson plan. What happened in those three months? A universal Social and Emotional Learning program with a mindfulness component was introduced to the entire school. The teachers play an important role in delivering the curriculum for this program. There are several options for delivering mindfulness-based programs in schools and information about diverse programs is offered in the first section of this chapter.

School-Based Universal Mindfulness Programs
A number of school-based mindfulness programs for adolescents are offered on a universal basis; these are typically social and emotional learning (SEL) programs with a mindfulness component (Meiklejohn et al., 2012). Some of these programs have been exposed to investigation and an overview of selected programs supported by research are discussed in this section of the chapter. These programs include the Mind-up program, the Learning to BREATHE program (L2B), the Mindfulness in Schools Project and .b program, and the Mindful Schools program. Selected unique programs that have been designed for use in particular schools also are discussed.

The MindUP Program
The MindUP program, a school-based SEL program with a mindfulness component, is an initiative of the Hawn Foundation (http://thehawnfoundation.org/about-us/). The program was developed with children and pre- and early adolescents in mind and is taught by teachers. The program supports self-regulation and incorporates neuroscience in the development of a curriculum based on lessons for students in Pre-K through 8th grade. There are 15 lessons in the Grade 6–8 curriculum emphasizing mindfulness skills, cognitive practices such as perspective-taking, and kindness. The curriculum also includes three daily sessions of experiential exercises in mindful attention training (the core practice) (Hawn Foundation, 2011). The 15 lessons are outlined in Table 4.1.

An early form of the MindUP program was the focus of a quasi-experimental study in US schools for 4th to 7th grade students between

Table 4.1 MindUP Curriculum. Grades 6–8

Hawn Foundation (2011)

Unit I: Getting Focused (Lessons 1–3) brain physiology and introduction of daily core practice of mindful attention	
Lesson 1	How Our Brains Work
Lesson 2	Mindful Awareness
Lesson 3	Focused Awareness: The Core Practice
Unit II: Sharpening Your Senses (Lessons 4–9) sensation, movement and cognition	
Lesson 4	Mindful Listening
Lesson 5	Mindful Seeing
Lesson 6	Mindful Smelling
Lesson 7	Mindful Tasting
Lesson 8	Mindful Movement I
Lesson 9	Mindful Movement II
Unit III: It's All About Attitude (Lessons 10–12) mind-set, learning, and happiness	
Lesson 10	Perspective Taking
Lesson 11	Choosing Optimism
Lesson 12	Appreciating Happy Experiences
Unit IV: Taking Action Mindfully (Lessons 13–15) mindful behaviors, community, the world	
Lesson 13	Expressing Gratitude
Lesson 14	Performing Acts of Kindness
Lesson 15	Taking Mindful Action in the World

the ages of 9 and 13 years (Schonert-Reichl & Lawlor, 2010). The study, with 246 participants, employed a waitlist control design in six intervention classrooms and six comparison classrooms. Students who participated in the intervention group showed increases in optimism, from pretest to posttest, compared to the comparison group. In addition, those in the intervention group showed improvements on teacher ratings of self-concept. Preadolescents showed more positive benefits for self-concept than did early adolescents (Schonert-Reichl & Lawlor, 2010).

In another study, the MindUP program was subjected to a randomized controlled trial with 4th and 5th grade students between 9 and 12 years of age. The study, with 99 participants, was conducted in four schools in a suburban public school district in Canada with random assignment of two classrooms to the MindUP program and two classrooms to the school district-sponsored social responsibility program (Schonert-Reichl et al., 2015). The MindUP program curriculum was delivered by the classroom teachers. Twelve weekly lessons, of approximately 40–50 minutes' duration, were completed and core mindfulness practices (i.e., focus on the breath and listening to a sound) were also offered to the participants on school days with three 3-minute practices daily. Weekly lessons incorporated activities such as mindful smell and taste, development of empathy, and learning optimism and gratitude. Activities that encouraged development of prosocial skills through kindness to peers and through community service were used. Teachers also were asked to incorporate the skills during the school day. Participants in the control group were assigned to a social responsibility program and engaged in the typical curriculum used in the school district. Students were taught a shared responsibility model involving learning to solve problems through peaceful means and respect of others based on democratic values and a sense of community within the classroom and school (Schonert-Reichl et al., 2015).

Study outcome measures included executive functioning (EF), collection of cortical samples, self-reports of well-being and prosocial behavior, feedback on peer prosocial behavior, and mathematics grades (Schonert-Reichl et al., 2015). On one measure of EF, the students in the MindUP group performed faster on posttest measures of reaction time than did the students in the comparison group. While students in the MindUP group showed different patterns of cortisol levels (an indication of physiological stress) compared to the responsibility group, the findings did not offer a clear interpretation of stress levels. Regarding psychological variables, students in the MindUP group showed greater posttest improvements in empathy, perspective-taking, optimism, emotional control, school self-concept, and mindfulness. Students also showed decreased depressive symptoms (compared to the social responsibility group). Initial differences were found between the two groups on pretest measures of peer-nominated prosocial and aggressive behaviors and peer liking with children in the MindUP condition actually starting out with poorer scores in these areas than the comparison group. Upon posttest, students in the MindUP group were more likely to improve from pretest to posttest on almost every dimension of peer-nominated prosocial behavior and those in the MindUP condition showed significant decreases in behavior problems from pretest to posttest for behavior related to breaking rules. Thus, the students in the MindUP program, when compared to students in the control group, showed greater improvements in biological and cognitive markers, showed greater improvements in mindfulness and a range of psychological factors, reported greater decreases in depression and aggression, and received higher ratings of prosocial behavior and peer acceptance (Schonert-Reichl et al., 2015).

The Learning to BREATHE (L2B) program

Another mindfulness-based curriculum specifically designed for universal delivery to adolescents is the Learning to BREATHE (L2B) program. Developed for classroom and group settings, the curriculum teaches stress management skills, promotes EF, cognitive, and academic skills, and emphasizes the development of kindness, gratitude, and compassion, and self-compassion skills for adolescents. It also uses discussions and activities directed toward practicing mindfulness in a group setting to help adolescents strengthen skills in attention and emotional regulation (Broderick & Frank, 2014). The six themes of L2B are represented by the "BREATHE" acronym which stands for body, reflections through thoughts, emotions, attention, tenderness, habits for a healthy mind, and empowerment (i.e., the overall goal of the program) (Broderick, 2013). These themes are incorporated into the curriculum through six or eighteen sessions, which are designed to be adapted to meet the needs of diverse groups. The six-session curriculum is offered in 45-minute sessions and may be better suited to those in Grades 8 or 9 –12, while those in Grades 5–8 or 9 may be better served through eighteen 15-minute sessions (Broderick, 2013). (See Table 4.2 for an overview of L2B themes and activities).

The L2B sessions are presented by teachers in a format that typically includes an introduction, group activities, and mindfulness (Broderick & Frank, 2014). The mindfulness practices are adaptations of those used in mindfulness-based stress reduction (MBSR; Kabat-Zinn, 1990); these practices include the body scan guided meditation, mindful movement, and awareness of the body, thoughts, and feelings. The program also incorporates loving kindness practice (Broderick & Frank, 2014). The L2B program meets the research criteria for effective SEL programs by

Table 4.2 Learning to BREATHE (L2B) Themes

Broderick (2013)	
B	Body: Mindful listening, eating, and walking
R	Reflection: Mindfully working with thoughts
E	Emotions: Understanding and working with feelings
A	Attention: Awareness of thoughts, feelings, and bodily sensations
T	Tenderness: Reducing harmful self-judgments
H	Habits for a healthy mind: Integrating mindful awareness into daily life
E	Empowerment: The goal of the program

the Collaborative for Academic, Social, and Emotional Learning Guide (http://learning2breathe.org/about/introduction).

The L2B curriculum, incorporated into mindfulness-based programs in schools, has been the focus of a number of studies. For example, Broderick and Metz (2009) reported on a pilot study of 120 twelfth-grade students in a US private Catholic high school that demonstrated several changes in outcome measures in the L2B group compared to a control group. Student self-reports showed decreased negative affect and decreased tiredness and aches and pain. Students also reported increased experiences of being more calm and relaxed and greater levels of self-acceptance and self-regulation. Another study in two public high schools in the suburban US found similar results for high school students (Metz et al., 2013). There were 129 students (mean age 16.5) in the L2B program and 87 students (mean age 16.4) in the comparison group (instruction-as-usual). Participants in the L2B group showed significantly lower levels of perceived stress and psychosomatic complaints when compared to the control group in a matched high school. In addition, the L2B group showed greater levels of affective regulation following participation in the program (Metz et al., 2013).

A more recent pilot study provided a modified L2B program to 27 ethnically diverse at-risk adolescents in grades 9–12 in a school-based mindfulness program in a US alternative high school setting (Bluth et al., 2016). Students were randomly assigned to an L2B program or a substance abuse control class. Students met once a week for 50 minutes over the course of one school semester. Participants were primarily from low-income families and the participants were predominantly Hispanic and African-American. Exercises included mindfulness of the body, thoughts, sounds, and emotions, walking meditation, the body scan, restorative yoga, attention exercises, and loving kindness exercises. The substance abuse classes, designed to address drug use and related concerns, were delivered according to a standardized format in a group setting. Analysis of pretest and posttest scores showed that the L2B participants showed greater improvements in depression than did the control participants. Also, changes favoring the L2B group were noted for social connectedness, mindfulness, and perceived stress.

The Mindfulness in Schools Project and the .b program

The Mindfulness in Schools Project (MiSP) is a universal manualized curriculum that promotes mental health, well-being, and social and emotional competence through techniques inspired by MBSR and mindfulness-based cognitive therapy (MBCT; Segal, Williams & Teasdale, 2002). Teachers are trained to deliver the curriculum through lessons taught in an interactive and experiential manner (Kuyken et al., 2013). The Mindfulness in Schools Project (MiSP) offers a mindfulness-based curriculum for children aged 7–9 years, called Paws b. A second program offers a 10-week format for adolescents aged 11–18 called the .b program (.b refers to the saying, "stop, breathe, and be") (https://mindfulnessinschools.org). An overview of the.b lessons is offered in Table 4.3.

The MiSP's .b curriculum was the focus of a study by Huppert and Johnson (2010) in which 155 boys aged 14 and 15 participated. Students were recruited from two independent (private) schools in the UK. The mindfulness-based training was offered in four weekly 40-minute classes. Discussions of awareness and acceptance were presented, and exercises such as walking meditation and mindfulness of the body, breathing, sounds, and thoughts were offered. Students in the mindfulness condition were given a CD with three audio files (8-minutes in length) of mindfulness exercises for personal use and asked to practice outside of the classroom. Participants in the control group attended regularly scheduled religious education sessions. Participants in both groups completed questionnaires prior to and following the intervention. No significant differences were found between the groups on mindfulness, resilience, or psychological well-being. However, in the mindfulness group, the amount of individual practice outside the classroom positively influenced improvement in psychological well-being and mindfulness. In addition,

Table 4.3 Mindfulness in Schools Project and the .b Curriculum. Ages 11–18

Session 1	An introduction to mindfulness
Session 2	Paying attention (training the muscle of your mind)
Session 3	Taming the animal mind (cultivating curiosity and kindness)
Session 4	Recognizing worry (noticing how your mind plays tricks on you)
Session 5	Being here now (from reacting to responding)
Session 6	Moving mindfully (movement with mindfulness)
Session 7	Stepping back (watching the thought-traffic of your mind)
Session 8	Befriending the difficult (dealing with difficult emotions)
Session 9	Taking in the good (being present with your heart)
Session 10	Pulling it all together (review the practices and look to the future)

https://mindfulnessinschools.org/what-is-b/nine-lessons/

improvement in well-being was related to agreeableness and emotional stability in the mindfulness group (Huppert & Johnson, 2010).

Another study of the .b program was conducted in the UK with 522 participants (ages 12–16 years). Participants in six schools (n=256) were offered the .b program, while students in six other control schools (n=266) received typical programs such as religious studies, or personal, social and health education (Kuyken et al., 2013). Schools included fee-paying (private) schools and public schools. Although there was no use of random assignment, pretest-posttest and 3-month follow-up data were collected. The MiSP curriculum was offered in an introductory session and eight additional weekly sessions taught by teachers in the intervention schools. Findings suggested that the .b program was well-received by participants, and that those who completed the .b program experienced decreased depressive symptoms (at both posttest and at follow-up), and increased sense of well-being and lower stress (at follow-up). In addition, students who reported greater levels of practicing mindfulness skills reported greater levels of well-being and less stress at follow-up (Kuyken et al., 2013).

Mindful Schools, The Inner Kids Program, and the Inner Resilience Program

The efficacy of other school-based programs incorporating mindfulness skills for adolescents also has been substantiated by research. For example, the Mindful Schools curriculum was used in a pilot study with random assignment of 18 ethnic minority children, ages 8–11 years, at a summer camp to either a health education control group or the Mindful Schools curriculum. Participants in the intervention group received ten 15-minute lessons from the Mindful Schools curriculum and showed reductions in depressive symptoms when compared to those exposed to the health education curriculum (Liehr & Diaz, 2010). The Mindful Schools curriculum also has been substantiated by research that has not been published to date; however, an overview of the findings is available. The study used a randomized-controlled design with 937 children in three public elementary schools in the US. The Mindful Schools curriculum, taught by 47 teachers, was offered and included 4 hours of mindfulness instruction. Students showed improvements in attention and participation in class activities when compared to the control group (http://www.mindfulschools.org/about-mindfulness/research/).

The Inner Kids program, developed by Susan Kaiser Greenland, is a mindful awareness program for children and adolescents. Participants are guided through various activities and exercises to enhance awareness of inner experience (e.g., thoughts, emotions, and body) and outer experiences (e.g., people and environment). This program is used in school and community settings (http://www.susankaisergreenland.com/inner-kids-program.html). There is research on the program with children (Flook et al., 2010), but no research to date with adolescents.

The Inner Resilience Program, founded by Director Linda Lantieri, offers workshops and retreats to help parents and educators learn skills to support personal balance. In addition, a curriculum for students in kindergarten through Grade 8, Building Resilience from the Inside Out, incorporates progressive muscle relaxation and mindfulness practices to help students learn how to build attention skills and practice methods for enhancing a calm and relaxed state (http://www.innerresilience-tidescenter.org/programs.html).

Unique universal school-based mindfulness programs

When funds supporting standardized programs are limited, or a flexible approach is required, tailoring a unique program may be warranted. Examples of these unique and flexible school-based mindfulness programs are offered to provide ideas for program development. Raes, Griffith, Van der Gucht, & Williams (2014) provided an adapted program, using aspects of MBCT (Segal et al., 2002) and MBSR (Kabat-Zinn, 1990) to provide a mindfulness program for 408 students in five schools in Belgium. Participants, ages 13–20 years, were randomly assigned by class to the mindfulness condition or control condition. An analysis was conducted on the posttest and 6-month follow-up data for the 88 participants who scored above the clinical cutoff for depression at baseline. Findings showed that these students showed significantly greater reductions in depression compared with the control group at the 6-month follow-up.

Unique programming also was used in a study of a mindfulness meditation (MM) program for students in an alternative high school in a rural community in the US (Wisner, 2014; Wisner & Norton, 2013). The study offered a universal 8-week school-based MM program to 35 high school students in grades 10–12 (Wisner, 2014). Students practiced MM twice a week in groups separated by grade level and twice a week with all students together. School personnel also participated in the meditation sessions.

Concept mapping (Trochim, 1989), a mixed-method approach, was used to collect and analyze the data. Data analysis yielded a number of perceived benefits of the program as identified by students. These benefits included enhanced self-awareness, emotional coping, and ability to pay attention. Benefits also included an improved state of mind, improved stress management, and more time spent being calm. Systemic benefits involved improved school climate and enhanced student engagement. Students identified the potential for MM to relieve stress and to improve school climate as particularly important for them (Wisner, 2014). In the same study, pretest-posttest teacher ratings showed improvements in student strengths (Wisner & Norton, 2013). For example, student affective strengths improved after participation in the program (e.g., identifies own feelings), as did school functioning (e.g., pays attention in class). Teacher ratings also showed student improvements in interpersonal strengths (e.g., uses anger management skills), and intrapersonal strengths (e.g., is self-confident), and family involvement (e.g., demonstrates a sense of belonging with family members) (Wisner & Norton, 2013).

School-Based Targeted Mindfulness Programs

Most of the school-based mindfulness programs for adolescents are offered on a universal basis, but there are some programs that are offered on a targeted basis. Rather than addressing a population of students, individual students are identified as appropriate for referral to a group program due to a particular need. These programs have incoporated MBSR, mindfulness-based stress reduction for teens (MBSR-T), mindfulness-based mixed martial arts, cognitive-behavioral therapy (CBT), and yoga interventions.

MBSR

In a targeted study of a school-based MBSR program in the US, low-income, urban, primarily African American participants were randomly assigned to the MBSR group (adapted for urban youth), or a comparison group. Participants were 7th and 8th grade boys (11–14 years of age). The 12-session MBSR group was offered to 22 participants, while 19 students participated in the health education comparison group. Pretest-posttest data analysis indicated that participants in the MBSR group showed less anxiety and rumination than those in the comparison group (Sibinga et al., 2013).

Table 4.4 MBSR-T. Ages 13–18

Edwards, Adams, Waldo, Hadfield, & Biegel (2014)	
Module 1	Examining Stress and an Introduction to Mindfulness
Module 2	Foundations of Mindfulness
Module 3	Working with What Is: Developing Practice and Present Moment Awareness
Module 4	Cultivating Self-Care and Awareness of Positive Experience
Module 5	Working with Thoughts and Unpleasant Events
Module 6	Coping Strategies, Letting Go, and Forgiveness
Module 7	Mindful Resilience
Module 8	Review and Intentions for the Future

MBSR-T

The mindfulness-based stress reduction for teens (MBSR-T) program incorporates a modified MBSR curriculum for adolescents and is delivered in a group format for weekly 50-minute sessions over 8 weeks (Biegel et al., 2009). The MBSR-T curriculum emphasizes informal mindful practices and awareness of thoughts. See Table 4.4 for an overview of the MBSR-T modules.

A targeted approach was used in a study of a school-based 8-session MBSR program for teens (Edwards, Adams, Waldo, Hadfield, & Biegel, 2014). Participants in this pilot study were 20 Latino middle school students, aged 12–17 years, in the rural US who participated in the 8-session structured after-school group program using the MBSR-T curriculum. Exercises included the body scan, sitting and walking meditation, yoga, and mindful homework and test taking. An audio CD also was used in conjunction with the program. Analysis of pretest-posttest data indicated that mindfulness and self-compassion scores increased while perceived stress and depression decreased for the MBSR-T participants (Edwards et al., 2014).

Integra Mindfulness Martial Arts Program

The Integra mindfulness martial arts (MMA) program incorporates mindfulness, (CBT), and mixed martial arts for adolescents seeking mental health treatment (Milligan et al., 2016). In a program offered in a school setting, the Integra MMA program was offered to 17 adolescents (13–17 years of age) once a week for 20 weeks (Milligan et al., 2016). Sessions lasted 1.5 hours and participants learned mindfulness techniques, participated in experiential exercises including the body scan, yoga, and martial arts, and learned about mindful self-talk. Participants in the program, compared to the waitlist control (n=18), showed improvements in secondary control (e.g., acceptance and positive thinking) and reductions in cognitive errors (e.g., catastrophizing) following the program (Milligan et al., 2016).

Unique School-Based Targeted Mindfulness Programs
Some studies of targeted programs explored practices developed specifically for particular populations. For example, Barnes and colleagues studied the physiological impact of a school-based meditation program for normotensive middle school students (Barnes, Davis, Murzynowski, & Treiber, 2004). Students (mean age 12.3 years) were randomly assigned, by classrooms, to either the meditation condition (n=34) or the health education control condition (n=39). The program lasted for three months and included both meditation sessions and instruction periods. The meditation practice was a breath awareness exercise (modeled on the introductory exercise in MBSR) and students participated in two daily 10-minute meditation sessions (one during school, one at home). Students also participated in a 20-minute instructional period once a week. Students assigned to the control condition participated in daily 20-minute walks and a weekly 20-minute education session about physical activity, weight loss, and dietary change. Compared to students in the control group, students in the meditation group showed decreased ambulatory heart rate, ambulatory systolic and diastolic blood pressure, and resting systolic blood pressure (Barnes, Davis et al., 2004).

In another study using the same intervention described by Barnes, Davis et al. (2004), participants were 121 African American students with high-normal systolic blood pressure. Participants were 9th grade students attending a US high school (Wright, Gregoski, Tingen, Barnes, & Treiber, 2011), and students were randomly assigned to one of three groups used in the study. Those in the meditation intervention group (n=35) participated in daily 10-minute breath awareness exercises. They also were asked to meditate for 10-minute sessions at home on weeknights and for two sessions on weekend days. Participants in the cognitive-behavioral life skills training group (n=42) participated in weekly 50-minute sessions which included group discussions and exercises such as modeling and behavioral rehearsal in solving problems, managing anger, and resolving conflict. They also participated in behavioral homework assignments. Those in the health education group (n=44) participated in weekly 50-minute lifestyle education sessions based on guidelines from the National Heart, Lung and Blood Institute. The programs were offered during health classes and continued for three months. Students in the breath awareness group showed reductions in blood pressure and hostility from pre-to post-intervention. Those in the life skills group showed reductions in hostility at the 3-month follow-up assessment.

The targeted approach also was used in a study of a school-based mindfulness and yoga intervention for youth in underserved urban communities. This program, created by founders of The Holistic Life Foundation (Ali Smith, Atman Smith, and Andres Gonzalez), integrates yoga, mindfulness, tai chi, and other healing modalities (http://hlfinc.org/services/urban-youth-yoga-mindfulness-training/). The 97 participants were fourth and fifth grade students attending four urban US public schools, and the schools were randomized to either the intervention or waitlist control condition. Following the 12-week intervention period, analysis of pretest-posttest data showed that students in the intervention groups, when compared with waitlist control groups, reported a decrease in rumination, intrusive thoughts, and emotional arousal (Mendelson et al., 2010). Furthermore, additional analysis showed that youth who reported lower levels of depressive symptoms at baseline showed decreased problematic stress responses when compared to the control youth (Gould, Dariotis, Mendelson & Greenberg, 2012).

Yoga also was the focus of an 8-week after-school program for fourth- and fifth-grade girls in two public schools in the US (White, 2012). Participants were randomly assigned to a weekly mindfulness-based yoga intervention (n=70) or a waitlist control group (n=85). The yoga program involved activities such as listening to meditation bells, sitting meditation, yoga, and discussion of experiences and homework assignments. Sessions were 1 hour in duration and participants were asked to complete 10 minutes of homework on a daily basis (e.g., stretching, sitting meditation, yoga postures, and relaxation). The yoga group reported increased appraisal of stress (i.e., how bad the child would feel if the stressor occurred) and greater frequency of coping scores compared to the control group.

Quach, Mano, and Alexander (2016) conducted a study in which 198 US junior high school students (ages 12–15 years) were randomly assigned to a MM condition (n=54 program completers), a hatha yoga condition (n=65 program completers), or to a waitlist control group (n=57 program completers). Students in the sitting MM condition and in the hatha yoga condition participated in the programs during physical education class periods for 45-minutes twice weekly for 4 weeks. Daily home practice of 15–30 minutes was encouraged and monitored. Results indicated that working memory capacity was found to improve following the MM condition but not for those in the hatha yoga or waitlist control conditions (Quach et al., 2016). All three groups showed significant reductions in stress and anxiety following the intervention period.

In another unique program, a mindfulness component was integrated into a comprehensive school-based suicide intervention program offered to eight Native American youth (ages 15–20 years) in a Bureau of Indian Education school in the US (Le & Gobert, 2015). The 10-week intervention was provided in a group format through four 55-minute sessions per week. Sessions included opening and closing cultural rituals, stories, and opportunities to engage in reflection. Also included were mindfulness practices, experiential activities, discussions, and homework assignments. Analysis of qualitative and quantitative data indicated a number of benefits. Students experienced improved attention and self-regulation with greater awareness and acceptance of thoughts and emotions. Students also reported fewer suicidal thoughts. Students reported that accessing silence, a quiet state, and nature were healing for them. The group intervention also was effective for facilitating relationships among students. This study offers a successful example of a mindfulness program integrated in a culturally sensitive manner to meet the needs of a Native American community.

In a targeted program in an elementary school in Hong Kong, sixth graders (n=20; ages 9–13) participated in a 9-week group mindfulness-based intervention (Lam, 2016). Students were chosen on the basis of a high level of internalizing problems (subclinical) and low level for externalizing problems. Students were randomly assigned to the intervention group or a waitlist control group. Posttests showed that those in the intervention group had decreased symptoms related to internalizing problems (i.e., worry, panic, obsessive compulsive disorder, and generalized anxiety).

Another targeted program was offered by Wisner and Starzec (2016). This qualitative study was conducted in a rural alternative high school in the US. A mindfulness-based program was specifically developed for 19 students in Grade 10 who were new to the school that year. Students participated in a 7-month school-based mindfulness skills program (including breath awareness, and seated, walking, and lying MM) integrated into the 10th grade curriculum. Students engaged in mindfulness practices twice weekly during class time, and completed initial questionnaires about their experiences and written journal entries based on their experiences in the program. They also completed final questionnaires upon completion of the program. In addition, at the completion of the program, 14 of the 19 program completers were individually interviewed. Intrapersonal and interpersonal benefits were identified from analysis of the journal entries and interviews. Intrapersonal benefits attributed to program participation included improvements in stress management, self-awareness, and self-regulation. Students also attributed the ability to reduce anger and manage anger more effectively to program participation. An increase in happiness from participation in the program was noted as were cognitive benefits including self-reported improvements in the ability to control thinking (e.g., decreased negative thoughts and increased beneficial thoughts), and to regulate thoughts. Improvements in sleep behavior and hygiene also were reported. Interpersonal benefits included themes of building relationships (with peers, family members, and teachers) and learning to trust (Wisner & Starzec, 2016).

School-Based Intensive Mindfulness Interventions

Rather than addressing a population of students or targeting students with particular needs for a group program, the intensive mindfulness intervention occurs at the individual level to help a student cope with personal challenges. Thus, MBIs for adolescents may be taught to particular adolescents by school personnel, such as teachers, counselors, social workers, psychologists, and nurses.

Summary: School-Based Mindfulness Programs

In summary, it is clear that school-based mindfulness programs offer a wide range of potential benefits for students within the theoretical frameworks of cognitive-behavioral theory, developmental neuroscience, and systems perspectives. These perspectives contribute to our understanding of how these practices bring about change for adolescents.

Mindfulness programs contribute to wellness through improvements in cardiovascular health and sleep hygiene. There also are many psychological benefits of these programs for students. For example, taking part in mindfulness practices promotes a sense of relaxation and calmness and contributes to stress management. Mindfulness practice also may promote strengths including heightened trust, perspective-taking, well-being, mindfulness, optimism, self-acceptance, self-confidence, self-awareness, self-compassion, and emotional coping. Likewise, mindfulness programs for adolescents promote executive functioning, attentiveness, and school functioning. Participation in these programs also contribute to increased happiness and reductions in depression, anxiety, and aggression. Likewise, greater levels of self-regulation are promoted often leading to improved anger management and reductions in behavior problems for adolescents.

Adolescents also may find that fostering mindfulness skills leads to a heightened ability to regulate intrusive thoughts and rumination. Culturally sensitive mindfulness-based programs may support students in this process. For example, finding a reduction in thoughts of suicide and worry may occur when adolescents are offered times to connect with nature and healing through mindfulness.

Adolescents may also find social benefits of participation in mindfulness-based programs including improved relationships with peers, family members, and teachers. Enhanced social connectedness and engagement, enhanced empathy, and greater levels of family involvement also may emerge from practicing mindfulness skills. School climate changes also may be observed as mindfulness programs are integrated into the school curriculum.

In addition to individual studies, meta-analytic and review studies of school-based mindfulness programs for children and adolescents provide strong support for the efficacy of these programs. Findings from a meta-analysis show that mindfulness-based interventions (MBIs) offered in school settings have the potential to improve cognitive performance and executive functioning, to enhance resiliency, and to reduce stress (Zenner, Herrnleben-Kurz, & Walach, 2014). The benefits of school-based mindfulness programs also are demonstrated in a systematic review by Felver, Celis-de Hoyos, Tezanos, and Singh (2016). The benefits noted in this review included increased mindfulness and improvements in physiological functioning. In addition, improved behavioral and emotional regulation through reductions in behavioral problems, anxiety, depression, and affective disturbances and suicidal ideation were reported. Also noted were improvements in positive affect, optimism, coping, and emotion regulation. Other benefits of the mindfulness programs included enhancements in social-emotional competence, social skills, classroom engagement, and classroom behavior.

Using mindfulness in schools is often provided through group interventions. However, there is great potential for school-based professionals to integrate mindfulness into their work with adolescents even in the absence of this type of program availability. The case scenario of Mia's Story illustrates how this approach could be integrated into a school setting. Those interested in mindfulness approaches may find resources in books and websites listed at the end of this chapter.

Mia's Story

Mia, a 15-year-old Mexican American girl lives with her parents and two younger brothers (John, 12 and David, 10) in their one-story home in San Antonio, Texas. Mia is in the tenth grade and attends school in her neighborhood high school in which 97% of students are of Mexican American ethnicity. Mia's mother has been diagnosed with breast cancer and is undergoing chemotherapy. Mia is worried about her mother and has been helping her father care for her two brothers.

Mia's math teacher, Mrs. Garcia, has noticed that Mia is tired in her morning math class, has developed some anxiety about her tests, and finds that her grades are dropping. Mrs. Garcia speaks with the school social worker, Mrs. Blanco who contacts Mia's parents and receives permission to have Mia seen for assessment in school. Ms. Blanco and Mia develop a rapport and she works with Mia to address her concerns. In talking with Mia, she finds that in addition to being tired and experiencing a drop in academic performance, Mia is having trouble concentrating and sleeping. Ms. Blanco contacts Mia's parents for additional information for a comprehensive psychosocial assessment. The information confirms Mia's primary concerns of anxiety about her mother's illness, insomnia, and dropping grades. Mia's parents accept assistance for themselves and grant permission for Ms. Blanco to help Mia in school.

Ms. Blanco starts a counseling relationship with Mia. Ms. Blanco thinks that mindfulness may be a helpful aspect of her work with Mia. Ms. Blanco had been introduced to mindfulness skills in her social work graduate classes some years ago and now has her own sustained mindfulness practice. She also has attended a number of workshops to learn to teach mindfulness skills. As part of the comprehensive service plan, Ms. Blanco introduces Mia to the concept of mindfulness and tells her how learning mindfulness skills could help her with her anxiety and insomnia. They also will monitor Mia's grades to see if reducing the anxiety and improving sleep will improve her grades.

Ms. Blanco begins to teach Mia how to use mindfulness techniques. They start with mindful breathing, relaxing the body, and learning acceptance and using a non-judgmental attitude. Mia begins using deep breathing, mindfulness, and acceptance skills during sessions with Ms. Blanco and soon is using the skills at home and in math class. She practices the skills when she meets with Ms. Blanco. Mia begins to feel less anxious as her parents get assistance for their needs and she uses the mindfulness skills to go to sleep at night and finds it easier to concentrate in school. Her grades are improving and she is beginning to feel more energetic. Mia spends time with her mother and has taught her mother how to use simple breathing and mindfulness skills to cope with her fatigue and medical treatments.

Mrs. Garcia begins to observe Mia's new approach to math and asks Ms. Blanco how she could use mindfulness to help the entire class. They convene an interdisciplinary meeting and include Mrs. Blanco, the school principal, and the guidance counselor. They agree to look for resources for integrating mindfulness into the classroom. They begin by doing an internet search and begin to collect information from organizations such as the Resilient Schools Program (http://www.bensonhenryinstitute.org/services/resilient-schools) and Mindful Schools (http://www.mindfulschools.org).

School-Based Meditation Programs

In addition to school-based mindfulness programs, there also are other types of meditation programs offered in schools. For example, the David Lynch Foundation offers support for providing Transcendental Meditation (TM) programming for adolescents in schools (https://www.davidlynchfoundation.org/pdf/Quiet-Time-Brochure.pdf), and Herbert Benson's (Benson, 1975) Relaxation Response (RR) method is a secular meditation approach offered in schools. In addition, the Center for Mind-Body Medicine (CMBM) offers school-based programs for students who have experienced trauma in their communities. Examples of these programs and information about the role they play in helping students are provided in subsequent sections of this chapter.

School-Based Universal Meditation Programs

Many school-based meditation programs are offered on a targeted basis, so there are a limited number of studies on universal school-based meditation programs. However, one type of universal program is supported through the Resilient Schools Program, under the auspices of the Benson-Henry Institute for Mind Body Medicine (BHI) at Massachusetts General Hospital. This program offers training to educators who learn mind/body self-care skills and learn to facilitate the program for students. The foundation of the program includes elicitation of the relaxation response (RR), and related skills and tools geared toward managing stress, improving health, and helping students perform better academically (see Table 4.5 for an overview of the exercises in the program).

A multi-year study of a universal RR program in a US middle school was conducted with primarily ethnic minority youth in an inner city

Table 4.5 The Resilient Schools Program

Stress awareness	Learn how chronic stress impacts capacity to learn
Dialogue on stress	Define stress and learn signs, symptoms, and solutions to stress
Relaxation Response	Learn about physiology of stress and relaxation response
Relaxation Response exercises	Learn deep breathing, body awareness, yoga, progressive muscle relaxation, mindfulness, and visualization
Goal setting	Set goals to maximize success
Decrease test anxiety	Learn to feel more in control in test situations
Coping skills	Learn coping skills to feel more in control of your life
Daily Life	Incorporate Relaxation Response into daily life
Training for implementation	Integrating mind/body interventions into schools and practice using and teaching skills

http://www.bensonhenryinstitute.org/services/resilient-schools

community marked by economic disadvantages (Benson et al., 2000). The average number of students in the school was 1753 for the 6, 7, and 8th grades over the course of the three-year intervention period. Teachers were trained to deliver the curriculum which included information about the physiology of stress, identification of personal stressors, and practice in the relaxation response method of meditation, body awareness, and mindfulness training. Since the curriculum was used over three years, some students received the curriculum for successive years, depending upon when they entered the school. Findings showed that higher grade point averages and work habit scores were reported for students with greater exposure to the RR curriculum. In addition, more exposure to the curriculum was related to greater improvement in classroom cooperation (Benson et al., 2000).

School-Based Targeted Meditation Programs

Targeted school-based meditation programs, both RR and TM, have been offered for students in particular grade levels or with particular challenges. An overview of the qualitative and quantitative studies that have been conducted on these programs is provided.

Relaxation Response

One of the first studies of meditation with adolescents that was reported in the scholarly literature was a quantitative study of the RR. The study employed a randomized experimental design with 50 high school sophomores in the US. Students were assigned to either the RR group with health education or the health education control group (Benson et al., 1994). Students in the RR group learned about stress management, nutrition, and drug use, and also received instruction in the RR (e.g., focusing attention, pacing the breath, relaxation, and maintaining a passive attitude). Classes met three times weekly for one semester with all sophomores eventually taking part in both conditions. Students in the curriculum group incorporating the RR showed significant increases in self-esteem and internal locus of control when compared to the health curriculum control group (Benson et al., 1994).

Another study of the RR was conducted on a program offered to US high school students in Grades 10 and 11. The RR was integrated into curriculum that included cognitive practices and relaxation exercises (Foret et al., 2012). Participants in the RR intervention group included 60 students in Grade 11, and 54 students in Grade 10 served in the waitlist control group. Participants represented approximately 15% of the students in Grades 10 and 11. Students took part in eight 45-min sessions offered over 4 weeks and were taught by trainers from the BHI. During each of the 8 sessions, students were led through a different technique to elicit the RR. These exercises included breath focus, mindfulness, meditation, progressive muscle relaxation, visualization, and yoga. Students also learned about stress, kept a gratitude journal, and engaged in exercises to address thinking patterns related to stress. Home practice was also recommended (5–10 minutes daily), and students had access to audio tracks to support this practice. Posttest analysis of data showed that students in the RR group reported a decrease in perceived stress and anxiety. Analysis of gender factors showed that the RR intervention was particularly helpful for girls, in terms of decreased anxiety, decreased perceived stress, and spiritual growth (Foret et al., 2012).

Transcendental Meditation

A targeted program used TM and was the focus of a qualitative study of a year-long school-based program for 10 US adolescents (ages 12–14 years) (Rosaen & Benn, 2006). Students practiced TM for two 10-minute sessions each school day. Themes that emerged from the data indicated that students reported benefits of increased emotional intelligence and improved academic performance as a consequence of meditation training. The students also indicated that meditation aided them in achieving a restful alertness and greater levels of concentration and energy. They also reported increased adaptability and improved emotional control, particularly with regard to anger. Students also reported increases in relaxation, patience, and tolerance as a result of their participation in the program (Rosaen & Benn, 2006).

In a series of three randomized studies of targeted school-based meditation programs, 362 high school students at three different schools in Taiwan participated in the meditation programs (So & Orme-Johnson, 2001). Outcome measures in all studies were the same and included assessments of fluid intelligence, information processing speed, practical intelligence, field independence, creativity, and state and trait anxiety.

In the first study, high school students (n=154, mean age of 16.5 years) were assigned to a TM group, a control group of students not interested in TM, or a waitlist control group that spent an equivalent time napping. Students in the TM group met with trained TM teachers who provided introduction lectures and personal instruction in the TM technique. These students were provided with 20-minute in-school sessions for practicing TM, while the comparison group spent an equivalent time napping. Students also were asked to practice TM or napping for a 20-minute session at home as well. The intervention continued for six months. Students in the TM group showed increased levels of practical intelligence, creativity, field independence, and speed of information processing and decreased levels of state and trait anxiety compared to students in the napping and no-interest control groups. Those in the TM group also showed improvements in fluid intelligence when compared to the no-interest control group. There were no differences in outcome measures between the napping and no-interest control groups.

In study 2, junior high school students (n=118) with a mean age of 14.6 years, were randomly assigned by class to a TM or a no-treatment control group. A third group of students comprised a contemplation meditation group and participated in a 5-day course to learn the contemplation meditation practice. Students were then provided with a 20-minute session for practicing TM or contemplation meditation during the school day and were asked to practice for 20 minutes at home as well. The program continued for a 6-month period of time. Students in the TM group showed increased levels of creativity, practical intelligence, information processing speed, and decreased levels of state and trait anxiety compared to the contemplation meditation group. There were no differences between these groups in fluid intelligence and field independence.

Students in the TM group outperformed the no-treatment control group on all outcome measures (fluid intelligence, information processing speed, practical intelligence, field independence, creativity, and state and trait anxiety). Students in the contemplation group out-performed participants in the no-treatment control group in field independence and information processing speed (So & Orme-Johnson, 2001).

In study 3, vocational high school students (n=99, mean age of 17.8 years) were randomly assigned by class to either a TM group or a no-treatment control group. The program continued for 12 months. Students in the TM group outperformed the no-treatment control group on all outcome measures (fluid intelligence, information processing speed, practical intelligence, field independence, creativity, and state and trait anxiety) (So & Orme-Johnson, 2001). Additional analyses calculated by combining the results for each variable across all three studies showed that TM had the strongest effects for creativity, practical intelligence, field independence, and state and trait anxiety (So & Orme-Johnson, 2001).

Barnes and colleagues offered a targeted 8-week school-based program to 35 high school students (34 African American and 1 Caucasian; 15–18 years old) who had high normal blood pressure readings. Participants were randomly assigned to a Transcendental Meditation (TM) condition (n=17) or to a control condition (n=18) (Barnes, Treiber, & Davis, 2001). The TM students received meditation instructions and were asked to practice twice daily for 15-minute sessions, with one of the 15-minute practice sessions taking place in school on school days. Students in the control group met for a weekly 1-hour lifestyle education session based on National Institute of Health guidelines for lowering blood pressure through weight loss, diet, and physical activity. The TM group, compared to the control group, showed reduced cardiovascular reactivity in response to acute stress and larger decreases in resting systolic blood pressure (Barnes, Treiber, &, Davis, 2001).

A school-based TM program in the US also was found to help students make behavioral changes (Barnes, Bauza, & Treiber, 2003). Participants were 45 African American high school students (15–18 years of age) with high-normal blood pressure who were randomly assigned by school to a Transcendental Meditation (TM) condition (n=25) or to a health control condition (n=20). Students in the TM group met with a meditation teacher and engaged in 15-minute in-school practice sessions on school days for 16 weeks. Students also were asked to practice after school and on weekends (15-minute sessions twice per day). Students in the control group met for daily 15-minute lifestyle education sessions on school days. Students who participated in the TM program showed fewer missed class periods, fewer rule violations, and fewer days suspended from school compared to the control group (Barnes, Bauza, & Treiber, 2003).

A similar targeted controlled study by Barnes and colleagues offered a school-based program to 100 African American high school students (mean age 16 years) with high-normal blood pressure who were randomly assigned by school to a Transcendental Meditation (TM) condition (n=50) or to a health control condition (n=50) (Barnes, Treiber, & Johnson, 2004). Students in the TM group met with a meditation teacher and engaged in 15-minute in-school practice sessions on school days for 16 weeks. Students also were asked to practice after school and on weekends (for 15-minute sessions twice daily). Students in the control group met for daily 15-minute cardiovascular health education sessions (partially based on National Institutes of Health guidelines) on school days. These sessions included information on managing weight through nutritional choices and increasing physical activity. The TM group, compared to the control group, showed reductions in day-time systolic and diastolic blood pressure. These findings were maintained at the 4-month follow-up (Barnes, Treiber, & Johnson, 2004).

In another study, a school-based targeted TM intervention was provided to 11 adolescents (ages 11–14 years) with attention deficit hyperactivity disorder (ADHD) (Grosswald et al., 2008). Students received instruction in the TM technique and practiced it in school for two 10-minute periods daily for three months. Teachers and administrators who had previously received TM instruction lead the meditation sessions. Students also were asked to continue the meditation sessions at home when school was not in session. At posttest, students showed decreased stress and anxiety as well as improvements in ADHD symptoms and executive function (Grosswald et al., 2008).

A targeted TM program was offered in a public urban middle school in the US (Nidich et al., 2011). The school served predominantly racial and ethnic minority students. Students were considered to be at-risk due to standardized test performance below proficiency level in English and math. Participants in the TM group (n=50) were in Grades 6 and 7 and practiced TM in school twice a day for three months. A matched control group of students in Grade 8 also was included in the study (n=50). Posttest findings showed that students in the TM group showed greater improvements on both English and math scores compared to students in the Grades 6 and 7 control group (Nidich et al., 2011).

The usefulness of TM for reducing psychological distress in racial and ethnic minority public high school students in four schools in the US was explored (Elder et al., 2011). One school was located in Connecticut (primarily serving African American students in an urban setting), one school was located in South Dakota (primarily serving American Indian students in a rural setting), and two schools were located in Arizona (primarily serving Hispanic students in an urban setting). Students self-selected into a TM group (n= 68) or a control group (n=38 students). The average age of the participants was 16.6 years. Students in the TM group were taught the technique by certified teachers and then practiced meditation twice a day for 10–15 minutes and were encouraged to keep the same practice regimen on the weekends. The control group spent an equivalent time in school resting, sitting quietly, reading, or working on homework while the TM group meditated. The meditation program continued for a 4-month period. Those in the TM group showed improvements in psychological distress (reductions in emotional symptoms) and anxiety compared to those in the control group. Within group decreases in anxiety were found for both the TM group and the control group.

Center for Mind-Body Medicine

A school-based application of the CMBMs mind-body skills group program was provided to 139 Kosovar adolescents (12–19 years of age) from a community exposed to war trauma (Gordon, Staples, Blyta, & Bytyqi, 2004). Teachers employed in the school and trained by the CMBM program taught the group sessions. The program sessions were offered in 3-hour sessions over the course of six weeks. Experiential activities included relaxation techniques, meditation and movement activities, guided imagery, and autogenic training. Other activities included simple biofeedback exercises, exploration of the family constellation through diagramming, and drawing exercises. Group support was promoted and participants were encouraged to share their experiences with each other. Data analysis indicated reductions in PTSD scores for participants following the mind-body skills groups (Gordon et al., 2004).

A second CMBM school-based study was conducted with 82 Kosovar adolescents (Gordon, Staples, Blyta, Bytyqi, & Wilson, 2008). Students were randomly assigned to a 12-session mind-body group program or a waitlist control group. High school teachers facilitated the group sessions that included experiential activities including breathing techniques, meditation and movement activities, guided imagery, and autogenic training. Other activities included simple biofeedback exercises, exploration of the family constellation through diagramming, and drawing exercises. Findings showed that participants in the intervention group, compared to the waitlist control group, had lower PTSD symptom scores at posttest (Gordon et al., 2008).

School-Based Intensive Meditation Interventions

Similar to MBIs in schools, there is limited literature about incorporating meditation as an intensive school-based intervention. However, the RR exercises could easily be adapted for use with individual adolescents and could be taught to adolescents by school-based professionals including teachers, social workers, counselors, psychologists, and nurses. On the other hand, it is not likely that TM would be taught in the same manner (i.e., outside of the grant-sponsored programs) in secular settings because of the nature of the fee process and the need for guidance from a certified instructor.

Summary: School-Based Meditation Programs

In summary, school-based meditation programs have the potential to help adolescents in a variety of ways. For example, participation in these programs may promote wellness through lowering blood pressure, reducing cardiovascular reactivity in response to stress, reducing symptoms of PTSD, and increasing feelings of energy. A sense of relaxation and restful alertness may be experienced with a decrease in perceived stress.

These programs also may foster adaptability, patience, self-esteem, and practical and emotional intelligence in adolescents. In addition, adolescents may notice increased levels of concentration, creativity, information processing speed, and enhanced academic performance with participation in meditation practices and programs. Enhanced emotional and behavioral self-regulation may result in fewer outbursts of anger and less anxiety. School-related behavioral infractions may be reduced. Social benefits of meditation programs for adolescents may result in greater tolerance toward others and cultural factors may include the promotion of spiritual growth.

The influence of developmental neuroscience, cognitive-behavioral theory, and cultural factors are evident in the physiological, psychological, cognitive, and social benefits of these programs and practices for students. As these benefits manifest in the adolescent's life, they may find personal strengths that foster a new sense of themselves and the possibilities of their lives. Those interested in learning more about these meditation approaches may find resources in books and websites listed at the end of this chapter.

Summary

It is clear from the emerging evidence reviewed in this chapter that school-based mindfulness and meditation programs are helpful for addressing a wide range of strengths and concerns for adolescents. Adolescents are learning how to regulate their emotions and behavior and often face challenges related to emotions of fear, anger, and sadness and self-defeating behaviors. Many students also have learning, emotional, and social challenges. Meditation as a practice technique has the potential to help students improve coping and increase self-awareness and manage behavior, thinking, and emotions a way that can help them succeed at home, at school, and in other settings. The benefits of these programs encompass the bio-psycho-social-cultural benefits discussed in Chapter 3.

These mindfulness and meditation practices and programs may be adapted in ways that provide effective programming without compromising benefits to students. Meditation practices vary and duration of meditation practice may be adjusted to meet the unique needs of students and settings. Moreover, the programs reviewed showed promise across a variety of settings (e.g., public schools, alternative schools, private schools, vocational schools), and in diverse countries (e.g., Canada, Hong Kong, the UK, the US). In addition, the utility and adaptability of using meditation in schools using a variety of techniques (e.g., mindfulness, TM, the RR, and the CMBM's program) has been established. It is clear that the cognitive-directed methods of meditation as described by Nash and Newberg (2013) predominate in educational settings (e.g., mindfulness).

Many of the studies examined here are pilot studies and preliminary projects as is common in an emerging field of study. As such, it is not always clear how to examine the effects of various components of a particular practice or program. Now that a solid foundation for studying mindfulness and meditation practices in educational settings has been established, the quality of the studies will improve.

School personnel, including teachers, counselors, social workers, psychologists, and nurses, are charged with supporting student success. These professionals wish to promote emotional balance, positive thinking, focused attention, and engagement in learning for students. In addition, a well-managed classroom and an accepting school environment reduces stress and fosters belongingness. These are the keys to a successful school experience. School-based professionals may find mindfulness and meditation to be effective and efficient tools for promoting student strengths and for offering students an oasis of calm during the potentially chaotic school day.

Resources

	Books
Biegel (2010)	*The Stress Reduction Workbook for Teens: Mindfulness Skills to Help You Deal with Stress*
Broderick (2013)	*Learning to Breathe: A Mindfulness Curriculum for Adolescents to Cultivate Emotion Regulation, Attention, and Performance*
Greco and Hayes (2008)	*Acceptance and Mindfulness Treatments for Children and Adolescents: A Practitioner's Guide*
Greenland (2010)	*The Mindful Child: How to Help Your Kid Manage Stress and Become Happier, Kinder, and More Compassionate*
Lantieri & Goleman (2008)	*Building Emotional Intelligence: Techniques to Cultivate Inner Strength in Children*
Rechtschaffen (2014)	*The Way of Mindful Education: Cultivating Well-being in Teachers and Students*
Saltzman (2014)	*A Still Quiet Place: A Mindfulness Program for Teaching Children and Adolescents to Ease Stress and Difficult Emotions*
Saltzman (2016)	*A Still Quiet Place for Teens: A Mindfulness Workbook to Ease Stress and Difficult Emotions*
Schonert-Reichl and Roeser (2016)	*Handbook of Mindfulness in Education: Integrating Theory and Research into Practice*
	Websites
Association for Mindfulness in Education	http://www.mindfuleducation.org
American Mindfulness Research Association	https://goamra.org
Center for Mindfulness in Medicine, Healthcare, and Society	http://www.umassmed.edu/cfm/
Center for Investigating Healthy Minds	http://www.investigatinghealthyminds.org
Center for Mind-Body Medicine	https://cmbm.org

(*continued*)

(continued)

Collaborative for Academic, Social, and Emotional Learning (CASEL)	http://www.casel.org
Holistic Life Foundation	http://hlfinc.org/services/urban-youth-yoga-mindfulness-training/
The Inner Kids Program	http://www.susankaisergreenland.com/inner-kids-program.html
The Inner Resilience Program	http://www.innerresilience.com/index.html
Learning to BREATHE	http://learning2breathe.org
The Mindfulness in Schools Project	http://mindfulnessinschools.org
MindUP	http://thehawnfoundation.org
Mind and Life Institute	https://www.mindandlife.org
Mindful Schools	http://www.mindfulschools.org
The Quiet Time Program	https://www.davidlynchfoundation.org/schools.html
Resilient Schools Program	http://www.bensonhenryinstitute.org/services/resilient-schools

References

Barnes, V. A., Treiber, F. A., & Davis, H. C. (2001). Impact of Transcendental Meditation on cardiovascular function at rest and during acute stress in adolescents with normal blood pressure. *Journal of Psychosomatic Research*, *51*(4), 597–605.

Barnes, V. A., Bauza, L. B., & Treiber, F. A. (2003). Impact of stress reduction on negative school behavior in adolescents. Health and Quality of Life Outcome, *1* (10). DOI:10.1186/1477-7525-1-10

Barnes, V. A., Davis, H. C., Murzynowski, J. B., & Treiber, F. A. (2004). Impact of meditation on resting and ambulatory blood pressure and heart rate in youth. *Psychosomatic Medicine*, *66*(6), 909–914.

Barnes, V. A., Treiber, F. A., & Johnson, M. H. (2004). Impact of Transcendental Meditation on ambulatory blood pressure in African American adolescents. *American Journal of Hypertension*, *17*(4), 366–369.

Benson, H. (1975). *The Relaxation Response*. New York, NY: William Morrow.

Benson, H., Kornhaber, A., Kornhaber, C., LeChanu, M. N., Zuttermeister, P. C., Myers, P., & Friedman, R. (1994). Increases in positive psychological characteristics with a new relaxation-response curriculum in high school students. *The Journal of Research and Development in Education*, *27*(4), 226–231.

Benson, H., Wilcher, M., Greenberg, B., Higgins, E., Ennis, M., Zuttermeister, P. C.,… & Friedman, R. (2000). Academic performance among middle-school students after exposure to a relaxation response curriculum. *Journal of Research and Development in Education*, *33*(3), 156–165.

Biegel, G. M. (2010). *The stress reduction workbook for teens: Mindfulness skills to help you deal with stress.* Oakland, CA: New Harbinger Publications.

Biegel, G. M, Brown, K. W., Shapiro, S. L, & Schubert, C. (2009). Mindfulness-based stress reduction for the treatment of adolescent psychiatric outpatients: A randomized clinical trial. *Journal of Clinical and Consulting Psychology, 77,* 855–866.

Bluth, K., Campo, R. A., Pruteanu-Malinici, S., Reams, A., Mullarkey, M., & Broderick, P. C. (2016). A school-based mindfulness pilot study for ethnically diverse at-risk adolescents. *Mindfulness, 7*(1), 90–104. DOI:10.1007/s12671-014-0376-1

Broderick, P. C. (2013). *Learning to breathe: A mindfulness curriculum for adolescents to cultivate emotion regulation, attention, and performance.* Oakland, CA: New Harbinger Publications.

Broderick, P. C. & Frank, J. L. (2014). Learning to BREATHE: An intervention to foster mindfulness in adolescence. *New Directions in Youth Development, 142,* 31–44.

Broderick, P. C., & Metz, S. (2009). Learning to BREATHE: A pilot trial of a mindfulness curriculum for adolescents. *Advances in School Mental Health Promotion, 2*(1), 35–46.

Edwards, M., Adams, E. M., Waldo, M., Hadfield, O. D., & Biegel, G. M. (2014). Effects of a mindfulness group on Latino adolescent students: Examining levels of perceived stress, mindfulness, self-compassion, and psychological symptoms. *The Journal for Specialists in Group Work, 39*(2), 145–163.

Elder, C., Nidich, S., Colbert, R., Hagelin, J., Grayshield, L., Oviedo-Lim, D., … & Gerace, D. (2011). Reduced psychological distress in racial and ethnic minority students practicing the transcendental meditation program. *Journal of Instructional Psychology, 38*(2), 109–117.

Felver, J. C., Doerner, E., Jones, J., Kaye, N. C., & Merrell, K. W. (2013). Mindfulness in school psychology: Applications for intervention and professional practice. *Psychology in the Schools, 50*(6), 531–547.

Felver, J. C., Celis-De Hoyos, C. E., Tezanos, K., & Singh, N. N. (2016). A systematic review of mindfulness-based interventions for youth in school settings. *Mindfulness, 7*(1), 34–45.

Flook, L., Smalley, S. L., Kitil, M. J., Galla, B. M., Kaiser-Greenland, S., Locke, J., … & Kasari, C. (2010). Effects of mindful awareness practices on executive functions in elementary school children. *Journal of Applied School Psychology, 26* (1), 70–95.

Foret, M. M., Scult, M., Wilcher, M., Chudnofsky, R., Malloy, L., Hasheminejad, N., & Park, E. R. (2012). Integrating a relaxation response-based curriculum into a public high school in Massachusetts. *Journal of Adolescence, 35*(2), 325–332.

Gordon, J. S., Staples, J. K., Blyta, A., & Bytyqi, M. (2004). Treatment of Posttraumatic Stress Disorder in postwar Kosovo high school students using mind-body skills groups: A pilot study. *Journal of Traumatic Stress, 17*(2), 143–147.

Gordon, J. S., Staples, J. K., Blyta, A., Bytyqi, M., & Wilson, A. T. (2008). Treatment of posttraumatic stress disorder in postwar Kosovar adolescents using mind-body skills groups: A randomized controlled trial. *The Journal of Clinical Psychiatry*, 69(9), 1469–1476.

Gould, L. F., Dariotis, J. K., Mendelson, T., & Greenberg, M. (2012). A school-based mindfulness intervention for urban youth: Exploring moderators of intervention effects. *Journal of Community Psychology, 40*(8), 968–982.

Greco, L. A., & Hayes, S. C. (2008). *Acceptance & mindfulness treatments for children & adolescents: A practitioner's guide.* New Harbinger Publications.

Greenland, S. K. (2010). *The mindful child: How to help your kid manage stress and become happier, kinder, and more compassionate.* New York, NY: Simon and Schuster.

Grosswald, S. J., Stixrud, W. R., Travis, F., & Bateh, M. A. (2008). Use of the transcendental meditation technique to reduce symptoms of attention deficit hyperactivity disorder (ADHD) by reducing stress and anxiety: an exploratory study. *Current Issues in Education, 10(2)*. Retrieved from: http://cie.asu.edu/ojs/index.php/cieatasu/article/view/1569

Hawn Foundation (2011). MindUP curriculum: Grades 6–8. New York, NY: Scholastic.

Huppert, F.A. & Johnson, D. M. (2010) A controlled trial of mindfulness training in schools: The importance of practice for an impact on well-being. *The Journal of Positive Psychology*, 5(4), 264–274. DOI:10.1080/17439761003794148

Kabat-Zinn J. (1990). *Full catastrophe living: Using the wisdom of your body and mind to face stress, pain and illness.* New York: Delacorte.

Kuyken, W., Weare, K., Ukoumunne, O. C., Vicary, R., Motton, N., Burnett, R.,…& Huppert, F. (2013). Effectiveness of the mindfulness in schools programme: Non-randomised controlled feasibility study. *The British Journal of Psychiatry, 203*(2), 126–131.

Lam, K. (2016). School-based cognitive mindfulness intervention for internalizing problems: Pilot study with Hong Kong elementary students. *Journal of Child and Family Studies, 25*(11), 1–16.

Lantieri, L., & Goleman, D. P. (2008). *Building emotional intelligence: Techniques to cultivate inner strength in children.* Boulder, CO: Sounds True.

Le, T. N., & Gobert, J. M. (2015). Translating and implementing a mindfulness-based youth suicide prevention intervention in a Native American community. *Journal of Child and Family Studies, 24*(1), 12–23.

Liehr, P., & Diaz, N. (2010). A pilot study examining the effect of mindfulness on depression and anxiety for minority children. *Archives of Psychiatric Nursing, 24* (1), 69–71.

Meiklejohn, J., Phillips, C., Freedman, M. L., Griffin, M. L., Biegel, G., Roach, A., ... Saltzman, A. (2012). Integrating mindfulness training into K–12 education: Fostering the resilience of teachers and students. *Mindfulness*, *3*(4), 291–307. DOI:10.1007/s12671-012-0094-5

Mendelson, T., Greenberg, M. T., Dariotis, J. K., Gould, L. F., Rhoades, B. L., & Leaf, P. J. (2010). Feasibility and preliminary outcomes of a school-based mindfulness intervention for urban youth. *Journal of Abnormal Child Psychology*, *38*(7), 985–994.

Metz, S., Frank, J. L., Reibel, D., Cantrell, T., Sanders, R., & Broderick, P. C. (2013). The effectiveness of the learning to BREATHE program on adolescent emotion regulation. *Research in Human Development*, *10*(3), 252–272. DOI: 10.1080/15427609.2013.818488

Milligan, K., Irwin, A., Wolfe-Miscio, M., Hamilton, L., Mintz, L., Cox, M., ... & Phillips, M. (2016). Mindfulness Enhances Use of Secondary Control Strategies in High School Students at Risk for Mental Health Challenges. *Mindfulness*, *7*(1), 219–227.

Nash, J. D. & Newberg, A. B. (2013). *Toward a unifying taxonomy and definition for meditation*. Jefferson Myrna Brind Center of Integration Medicine Faculty Papers. Paper 11. http://jdc.jefferson.edu/jmbcimfp/11

Nidich, S., Mjasiri, S., Nidich, R., Rainforth, M., Grant, J., Valosek, L., ... & Zigler, R. (2011). Academic achievement and transcendental meditation: A study with at-risk urban middle school students. *Education*, *131*(3), 556–564.

Quach, D., Mano, K. E. J., & Alexander, K. (2016). A randomized controlled trial examining the effect of mindfulness meditation on working memory capacity in adolescents. *Journal of Adolescent Health*, *58*(5), 489–496.

Raes, F., Griffith, J. W., Van Der Gucht, K., & Williams, J. M. G. (2014). School-based prevention and reduction of depression in adolescents: A cluster-randomized controlled trial of a mindfulness group program. *Mindfulness*, *5*(5), 477–486.

Rechtschaffen, D. (2014). *The way of mindful education: Cultivating well-being in teachers and students.* New York, NY: WW Norton & Company.

Rosaen, C. & Benn, R. (2006). The experience of Transcendental Meditation in middle school students: A qualitative report. *Explore*, *2*(5), 422–425.

Saltzman, A. (2014). *A Still Quiet Place: A mindfulness program for teaching children and adolescents to ease stress and difficult emotions.* Oakland, CA: New Harbinger Publications.

Saltzman, A. (2016). *A Still Quiet Place for teens: A mindfulness workbook to ease stress and difficult emotions.* Oakland, CA: New Harbinger Publications.

Schonert-Reichl, K. A., & Lawlor, M. S. (2010). The effects of a mindfulness-based education program on pre-and early adolescents' well-being and social and emotional competence. *Mindfulness*, *1*(3), 137–151.

Schonert-Reichl, K. A., & Roeser, R. W. (2016). *Handbook of Mindfulness in Education: Integrating Theory and Research into Practice.* New York, NY: Springer.

Schonert-Reichl, K. A., Oberle, E., Lawlor, M. S., Abbott, D., Thomson, K., Oberlander, T. F., & Diamond, A. (2015). Enhancing cognitive and social-emotional development through a simple-to-administer mindfulness-based school program for elementary school children: A randomized controlled trial. *Developmental Psychology, 51*(1), 52–66.

Segal, Z. V., Williams, J. M. G., & Teasdale, J. D. (2002). *Mindfulness-based cognitive therapy for depression: A new approach to relapse prevention*. New York, NY: Guilford.

Sibinga, E. M. S., Perry-Parrish, C., Cheung, S., Johnson, S. B., Smith, M., & Ellen, J. M. (2013). School-based mindfulness instruction for urban male youth. A small randomized controlled trial. *Preventative Medicine, 57*(6), 799–801. DOI:10.1016/j.ypmed.2013.08.027

So, K., & Orme-Johnson, D. (2001). Three randomized experiments on the longitudinal effects of the Transcendental Meditation technique on cognition. *Intelligence, 29*, 419–440.

Trochim, W. M. (1989). An introduction to concept mapping for planning and evaluation. *Evaluation and Program Planning, 12*(1), 1–16.

White, L. S. (2012). Reducing stress in school-age girls through mindful yoga. *Journal of Pediatric Health Care, 26*(1), 45–56. DOI:10.1016/j.pedhc.2011.01.002

Wisner, B. L. (2014). An exploratory study of mindfulness meditation for alternative school students: perceived benefits for improving school climate and student functioning. *Mindfulness, 5*(6), 626–638.

Wisner, B. L., & Norton, C. L. (2013). Capitalizing on behavioral and emotional strengths of alternative high school students through group counseling to promote mindfulness skills. *The Journal for Specialists in Group Work, 38*(3), 207–224.

Wisner, B. L., & Starzec, J. J. (2016). The process of personal transformation for adolescents practicing mindfulness skills in an alternative school setting. *Child and Adolescent Social Work Journal, 33*(3), 245–257.

Wright, L. B., Gregoski, M. J., Tingen, M. S., Barnes, V. A., & Treiber, F. A. (2011). Impact of stress reduction interventions on hostility and ambulatory systolic blood pressure in African American adolescents. *Journal of Black Psychology, 37*(2), 210–233.

Zenner, C., Herrnleben-Kurz, S., & Walach, H. (2014). Mindfulness-based interventions in Schools: A systematic review and meta-analysis. *Frontiers in Psychology, 5*(603), 1–20. http://dx.doi.org/10.3389/fpsyg.2014.00603

CHAPTER 5

Mindfulness for Adolescents in Counseling, Behavioral Health, and Medical Settings

Introduction

Adolescents may encounter any number of personal stressors and health challenges as they grow into emerging adulthood. Specialized programs are offered to provide treatment for adolescents with medical and behavioral health concerns including substance abuse and addiction. Mindfulness-based interventions (MBIs) to help adolescents cope with these challenges have been introduced in outpatient and inpatient settings through personal, group, and family counseling. Synthesis of this literature was included in Chapter 3 and examples of these programs in educational settings were presented in Chapter 4. This chapter offers examples of selected studies that support the efficacy of using mindfulness interventions in clinical and medical settings. The focus is on mindfulness approaches since there is scant literature about other meditation interventions (such as the Center for Mind-Body Medicine's program, Transcendental Meditation, and the Relaxation Response) for adolescents in counseling, behavioral health, and medical settings.

Therefore, the MBIs discussed in this chapter include mindfulness-based stress reduction (MBSR; Kabat-Zinn, 1990), mindfulness-based cognitive therapy (MBCT; Segal, Williams, & Teasdale, 2002), dialectical behavior therapy (DBT; Linehan, 2014), and acceptance and commitment therapy (ACT; Hayes, Strosahl, & Wilson, 2012). In addition, adaptations of these programs for adolescents are discussed; these programs include mindfulness-based stress reduction for teens (MBSR-T;

B.L. Wisner, *Mindfulness and Meditation for Adolescents*,
DOI 10.1057/978-1-349-95207-6_5

Biegel et al., 2009), mindfulness-based cognitive therapy for children (MBCT-C; Semple et al., 2010), dialectical behavior therapy for adolescents (DBT-A; Rathus & Miller, 2014), and ACT for adolescents (Greco, Blomquist, Acra, & Moulton, 2008). This chapter also includes a case example to illustrate the application of a mindfulness-based program for adolescents in a behavioral health setting.

Mindfulness-Based Interventions

As mentioned, MBIs for use in clinical settings with adolescent clients or patients are often derived from MBSR, MBCT, DBT, and ACT (Baer, 2014). Programs have been developed to meet the unique developmental needs of adolescents in outpatient and inpatient settings. Some of those programs are closely based on MBSR (e.g., MBSR-T with mindfulness as a primary skill) while others combine cognitive-behavioral concepts with mindfulness skills (e.g., MBCT-C). Other practices and programs adapt cognitive-behavioral theory and use mindfulness skills as one component of treatment (e.g., DBT-A and ACT for adolescents).

Interventions Adapted from Mindfulness-Based Stress Reduction

Mindfulness-based stress reduction uses mindfulness training, yoga, and experiential exercises to reduce stress and symptoms of various medical concerns in adults (Kabat-Zinn, 1990). This intervention has been adapted for children and adolescents and examples of MBSR programs adapted for adolescents in behavioral health and medical settings in the US are offered here (e.g., Biegel, Brown, Shapiro, & Schubert, 2009; Bootzin & Stevens, 2005; Sibinga, Kerrigan, Stewart, Johnson, Magyari, & Ellen, 2011). Programs using mindfulness meditation (MM) also have been used in these behavioral health and medical settings (Haydicky, Wiener, Badali, Milligan, & Ducharme, 2012; Van de Weijer-Bergsma, Formsma, de Bruin, & Bögels, 2012).

Mindfulness-based stress reduction was used as one aspect of treatment for 55 adolescents with sleep disturbances in an outpatient substance abuse treatment setting (Bootzin & Stevens, 2005). Participants, aged 13–19 years, were offered six weekly 90-minute sessions that included education about sleep behavior and how to improve sleep, use of bright light to assist with sleep behavior, cognitive restructuring, and MBSR. Analysis of participant sleep diaries for those who completed 4 of the 6 sessions (N=23) indicated improvements in the quality of sleep (Bootzin & Stevens, 2005).

An 8-week MBSR-T group program was offered in addition to the typical psychological treatment for adolescents receiving outpatient treatment in a psychiatric hospital (Biegel et al., 2009). Modifications to the MBSR curriculum included reduction of time recommended for at-home practice sessions, no day-long retreat, and tailoring the presentation and discussion topics to focus on content relevant to adolescents. An overview of the modules for MBSR-T was provided in the previous chapter (Table 4.4).

The adolescents, aged 14–18 years, were diagnosed with a variety of concerns, including mood and anxiety disorders, parent-child problems, and problems related to abuse or neglect. They participated in sitting and walking meditation, the body scan, and yoga exercises. Participants also discussed their experiences and learned how to integrate the practices into daily life with practice at home being encouraged. Data were analyzed from the 74 adolescents who completed the program. Findings indicated that, when compared to the waitlist control group, participants in the MBSR program experienced increased self-esteem, improved quality of sleep, and reductions in anxiety, depression, and physical symptoms (Biegel et al., 2009).

An MBSR program also was offered for African American at-risk urban youth (13–21 years of age) in a hospital pediatric and adolescent outpatient clinic (Sibinga et al., 2011). Of the 26 youth, 11 were diagnosed with the human immunodeficiency virus (HIV). Four separate MBSR groups were conducted with two groups composed of participants diagnosed as HIV positive. There were no control groups, and each group received nine weekly sessions of MBSR content including presentation of information about topics such as mindfulness and meditation, experiential exercises including mindfulness and yoga, and group discussion tailored to meet the needs of the adolescent participants. Modifications included changes in length of the sessions and support appropriate for adolescents (e.g., helping with transportation concerns and offering snacks during the programs).

Analysis of quantitative and qualitative data showed reductions in hostility, perceived stress, general discomfort, and emotional discomfort following participation in the program. Also noted were improvements in relationships, school achievement, and physical health. In addition, improved medication adherence was reported for participants diagnosed as HIV positive (Sibinga et al., 2011).

Thus, we see that interventions adapted from MBSR have the potential to bring healing to youth, and also support coping for youth being treated in clinical outpatient programs in diverse settings. The theories that provide a foundation for these programs include developmental neuroscience, cognitive-behavioral theory, and systems and ecological perspectives. This is reflected in the literature showing psychological benefits of these programs to include increased emotional self-regulation, self-esteem, and school achievement. In addition, benefits included reduced stress, anxiety and depression, and changes in thoughts and behaviors. Social benefits related to improvements in relationships also were noted in the research on interventions adapted from MBSR.

Other Mindfulness-Based Programs for Adolescents

Programs using mindfulness training and other techniques also have been adapted for adolescents in outpatient and inpatient settings (Haydicky et al., 2012; Singh et al., 2007; Van de Weijer-Bergsma et al., 2012). For example, an MBI called *Meditation on the Soles of the Feet* has been used to help US adolescents diagnosed with a variety of conditions, including conduct disorder. In this technique, practitioners learn a mindfulness practice combining acceptance of emotions and redirection of attention to the sensations in the soles of the feet. The purpose of the practice is to reduce arousal levels in potentially stressful circumstances while also increasing behavioral flexibility (Singh et al., 2007).

This technique, following individual instruction and guidance, was shown to reduce aggression in adolescents at risk of expulsion from school due to aggressive behaviors associated with conduct disorder (Singh et al., 2007). In this study, three middle school adolescents diagnosed with conduct disorder were referred from school for outpatient therapy to address aggressive behavior. These students (aged 13–14 years) were at risk of being expelled from middle school if the behavior was not modified. A therapist met individually with each adolescent for three 15-minute sessions per week for four weeks. The first session was an introductory session and the second session included training in the meditation technique. Subsequent training sessions involved practicing the technique and gathering self-reports on behavior. Following 4 weeks of training, the adolescents met with the therapist once a month for 25 weeks for a discussion of the mindfulness practice and school behavior. Analysis of the baseline, training, and practice phases of the study showed that aggressive behavior decreased during the practice phase for all three adolescents. In addition, according to school records accessed at the follow-up phase, all three students graduated from middle school. The adolescents indicated that the mindfulness techniques were helpful for promoting relaxation and controlling their behavior (Singh et al., 2007).

Another evaluation of an MBI, for adolescents with learning disabilities (LD), was conducted at a children's mental health center in Canada (Haydicky et al., 2012). The outpatient intervention integrated mindfulness, mixed martial arts, and behavior modification, consistent with the 20-week manualized group program called the Mindfulness Martial Arts (MMA) program. Sixty participants, aged 12–18 years, were assigned to the intervention group or a waitlist control group (WL). Weekly 90-minute sessions included learning about mindfulness (e.g., acceptance and present moment awareness) and participation in experiential activities (e.g., developing meditation skills through mindfulness practice and mantra recitation, sitting and walking meditation, and the body scan). Also included in the sessions were activities related to cognitive-behavioral therapy, including learning to recognize and label thoughts, emotions, and bodily sensations and learning new coping skills (e. g., positive self-talk and reducing self-defeating thoughts and behavior). Home practice also was encouraged (Haydicky et al., 2012).

Data were analyzed by separating participants into various groups based on particular challenges. When the group with learning disabilities (LD) and attention deficit hyperactivity disorder (ADHD) was compared with the waitlist control group (14 MMA, 14 WL), it was found that the intervention group showed greater improvements in parent ratings of conduct and oppositional-defiant problems and externalizing behaviors than did the control group. Those participants with greater levels of hyperactive/impulsive symptoms (n=12) showed greater improvements in parent ratings of social problems and monitoring skills when compared to the control group (n=17). In addition, based on parent ratings, participants with elevated symptoms of inattention (n=15) showed greater improvements on social problems when compared to the waitlist control (n=18). Finally, boys with elevated anxiety (n=12) showed decreased anxiety at posttest, based on parent ratings, when compared with the waitlist control group (n=17) (Haydicky et al., 2012).

Another outpatient MBI was provided to 10 adolescents with ADHD in an outpatient community mental health setting in the Netherlands (Van de Weijer-Bergsma et al., 2012). The intervention consisted of an 8-week group mindfulness training for the adolescents and a Mindful Parenting group training for parents (N = 19). The program for adolescents consisted of weekly 90-minute sessions of mindfulness training (e.g., breathing meditations, sitting meditation, and body scan exercises) and homework assignments. Parent sessions consisted of mindfulness training with an emphasis on present moment awareness, nonjudgmental acceptance, and self-care. Parents learned mindfulness skills and also practiced choosing more effective responses to parenting circumstances rather than simply reacting to their child's behavior. Parents also received a CD with mindfulness exercises so they could practice mindfulness at home. The adolescents, their parents, and their tutors (N=7) completed measurements of adolescent behavior (Van de Weijer-Bergsma et al., 2012).

Findings indicated that adolescents showed declines in self-reported attention problems at the 8-week follow-up and showed improved performance on computerized tests of attention at posttest and the 8-week follow-up. Fathers also rated the adolescent as showing improved attention at the 8-week follow-up. Fathers rated the adolescent as showing improvements in externalizing behavior at posttest and at the 8-week follow-up. Also reported from the father ratings were reductions in problems related to executive functioning and behavioral regulation at the 8-week follow-up assessment. In addition, fathers reported less parenting stress at posttest and at the 8-week follow-up, but reported increased parental overreactivity at posttest. Alternatively, mothers reported decreased parental overreactivity at posttest (Van de Weijer-Bergsma et al., 2012).

In summary, preliminary research shows that unique mindfulness-based programs are helpful for adolescents treated in clinical outpatient therapy programs. Psychological benefits of these programs include emotional self-regulation changes (e.g., increased relaxation and decreased anxiety and aggressive behavior), cognitive changes (e.g., decreased attention problems and improved performance on tests of attention and executive functioning), and behavioral regulation changes (e.g., improvements in externalizing behaviors). In addition, fewer social problems were noted for adolescent participants following these programs.

Promotion of these benefits may be best understood in the context of developmental neuroscience, cognitive-behavioral theory, and the transtheoretical model of change. Benefits are optimized by understanding the timing of interventions to promote improvements in self-regulation of thoughts, behaviors, and emotions.

Interventions Adapted from Mindfulness-Based Cognitive Therapy

Mindfulness-based cognitive therapy incorporates aspects of mindfulness training and cognitive-behavioral therapy (CBT) to prevent recurrence of depression in adults (Segal, Williams, & Teasdale, 2002). This intervention has been adapted for children and adolescents and examples of studies of MBCT programs adapted for adolescents in behavioral health and medical settings are offered here (e.g., Ames, Richardson, Payne, Smith, & Leigh, 2014; Deplus, Billieux, Scharff, & Philippot, 2016; Semple, Lee, Rosa, & Miller, 2010; Bögels, Hoogstad, van Dun, DeShutter, & Restifo, 2008).

Mindfulness training (based on MBCT and adapted for use with adolescents) was offered to 14 adolescents (aged 11–18 years) with externalizing disorders (Bögels et al., 2008). These disorders (ADHD, oppositional-defiant disorder, and conduct disorder) are all characterized by deficits in behavioral control. The 8-week outpatient program was offered in 90-minute group sessions at a community mental center in the Netherlands, and parents also participated in a separate mindful parenting training group program. Adolescents engaged in mindful eating, walking, and listening exercises. They also engaged in breath awareness, body scan, yoga, and trust-building exercises. Incorporation of mindfulness into daily life was encouraged. Parents engaged in similar exercises along with opportunities to discuss communication, parenting, and personal goals.

Analysis of post-treatment data indicated that adolescents improved on personal goals, happiness, and mindful awareness and reported fewer internalizing and externalizing complaints and attention problems. The adolescents also performed better on a sustained attention test. Analysis of data for parents showed that parents recognized improvement on their own goals and in their child's goals. In addition, parent data showed that the adolescents experienced fewer externalizing and attention problems, increased self-control, and attunement to others following treatment. The data also showed that improvement for adolescents and parents was maintained at the 8-week follow-up period (Bögels et al., 2008).

One adaptation of MBCT is mindfulness-based cognitive therapy for children (MBCT-C; Semple et al., 2010). This intervention is a 12-session manualized group psychotherapy for children and adolescents (ages 9–13 years) experiencing anxiety and attention problems (Semple et al., 2010). MBCT-C extends the 8-week MBCT program to 12 weeks and uses 90-minute sessions (rather than 2-hour sessions). The mindfulness exercises are adapted to meet the developmental needs of children and adolescents.

For example, sensory exercises and games with brief activities and movement exercises are employed in MBCT-C rather than lengthier meditative practices and verbal interchanges used in MBCT. In addition, MBCT-C limits enrollment to 8 children with one or two therapists (rather than a maximum of 12 participants and one therapist with MBCT). Also, parents participate in various activities related to the treatment program (e.g., introductory sessions, mindfulness sessions, and joint home practice with their children) (Semple et al., 2010).

A randomized controlled trial was employed to assess the effects of an MBCT-C group intervention program for 25 participants (aged 9–13 years) in an inner city university outpatient clinic in the US (Semple et al., 2010). Participants primarily were from ethnic minority groups, lived in low-income neighborhoods, and were referred for the intervention based on academic problems (i.e., need for remedial reading). Some students also showed evidence of stress or anxiety at pretest. Participants engaged in the 12-week, 90-minute sessions with exercises and activities consistent with MBCT-C. These exercises included mindfulness activities, yoga, body scan, and guided imagery (Semple et al., 2010).

Analysis of data indicated that those who completed the program, compared to wait-list controls, showed reductions in attention problems at posttest and three-month follow-up. Reductions in behavior problems were associated with reductions in attention problems. Also, for those participants with initial levels of clinically elevated anxiety at pretest, a reduction in anxiety and improvements in behavior problems were reported at posttest (Semple et al., 2010).

Another study of an MBCT program adapted for use with adolescents was conducted with adolescents with mood disorders including depression and anxiety (Ames et al., 2014). The 8-week pilot study was offered to 11 adolescents (12–18 years of age) in two adolescent mental health settings in England, with seven participants completing the program (Ames et al., 2014). The 8-week program included information about mindfulness, mindfulness exercises including the body scan, mindful listening, seeing, smelling, and mindful movement. Time also was spent learning about acceptance, discriminating between thoughts, emotions, and behaviors, and finding ways to incorporate mindfulness into daily life (Ames et al., 2014). Analysis of qualitative data indicated that participants found increased awareness of thoughts and action with concomitant changes in relating to thoughts and feelings. Participants reported using mindfulness when feeling distressed. In addition, increases in mindfulness and quality of life also were reported as were reductions in depression, worry, and repetitive thoughts (Ames et al., 2014).

A program adapted from MBCT also was offered for adolescents at an academic center for clinical psychology in Belgium (Deplus et al., 2016). Although approximately 57% of the participants experienced mild depression, none of the adolescents were diagnosed with an acute mental health condition requiring psychiatric intervention. The outpatient group intervention, offered to 21 participants (11–19 years of age), was modified to include nine weekly sessions of 90-minute duration. The intervention did not focus on depression but included information about mindfulness, emotion, and emotion regulation. Experiential mindfulness techniques (e.g., listening to music and mindful breathing) were used and participants practiced being mindful of body sensations, attitudes, thoughts, values, and actions. The program also included homework and participants were provided with a CD to encourage use of mindfulness exercises at home. Posttest findings showed increased mindfulness and decreased depressive symptoms for participants. In addition, participants reported reductions in impulsive behavior and disruptive cognitive patterns (Deplus et al., 2016).

In summary, interventions adapted from MBCT may be used successfully with adolescents struggling with a variety of behavioral and emotional challenges including depression, anxiety, and externalizing behaviors. Psychological benefits of these interventions included emotional self-regulation changes (e.g., increases in self-control, reductions in impulsive behavior, reductions in depression and depressive symptoms, and reductions in anxiety) and improved quality of life. Cognitive changes included increased mindfulness, decreased attention problems, reductions in worry and repetitive thoughts, and increased awareness of thoughts and actions. Behavioral regulation changes included improvements in externalizing behaviors and fewer behavior problems. In addition, social benefits involved improved attunement to others following program participation. Conclusions from a meta-analysis of mindfulness interventions with youth lend support to these findings (Zoogman, Goldberg, Hoyt, & Miller, 2015). In particular, improvements in psychological symptoms for youth were noted from the meta-analysis. Theoretical perspectives most relevant to these programs in behavioral health and medical settings are developmental neuroscience, cognitive-behavioral theory, and the systems perspective.

Interventions Adapted from Dialectical Behavior Therapy

Dialectical behavior therapy (DBT) was originally developed to facilitate treatment for adults with co-occurring suicidal ideation, suicidal behavior, or nonsuicidal self-injurious behavior and a diagnosis of borderline personality disorder (BPD) (Linehan, 2014). A treatment manual is available and describes the components of DBT including training in mindfulness skills, interpersonal skills, emotion regulation skills, and distress tolerance skills. Those participating in DBT are offered individual therapy, group therapy, and telephone coaching (Linehan, 2014). Therapists also are supported through a coaching team. Early research showed that DBT was helpful for reducing suicidal ideation and associated behaviors and for reducing hospitalization in adults (Linehan, Armstrong, Suarez, Allmon, & Heard, 1991). More recently, DBT also has been successfully used for treatment of a wide range of disorders (e.g., eating disorders, depression, and problem drinking) (Linehan, 2014).

Dialectical behavior therapy also has been adapted for use with adolescents (dialectical behavior therapy for adolescents; DBT-A). This is a manualized program explained in detail in the treatment manual for DBT-A (Rathus & Miller, 2014). The components of DBT-A include weekly individual therapy, family therapy as required by the particular adolescent, and multifamily skills training. Sessions include training in skills including mindfulness, interpersonal effectiveness, distress tolerance, emotional regulation, and family communication. Regular phone contact between the individual therapist and the patient is a crucial aspect of DBT-A (Rathus & Miller, 2014).

A meta-analysis of studies of DBT with adolescents, while addressing the methodological limitations of current studies, suggested that DBT is a promising approach for those with nonsuicidal self-injury and depression (Cook & Gorraiz, 2016). In addition, MacPherson, Cheavens and Fristad (2013) offer a compelling discussion of the theoretical, treatment, and empirical underpinnings of DBT with adolescents. Examples of DBT programs adapted for use with adolescents in behavioral health and medical settings are available in the literature and are discussed here (e.g., Fleischhaker, Böhme, Sixt, Brück, Schneider, & Schulz, 2011; Goldstein, Axelson, Birmaher, Brent, 2007; Katz, Cox, Gunasekara, & Miller, 2004; Rathus, & Miller, 2002).

A study using DBT was conducted in an outpatient treatment program for urban US adolescents, largely from Hispanic ethnic groups, with a diagnosis of borderline personality disorder (BPD) (or a minimum of three features of BPD) and co-occurring suicidal ideation (Rathus & Miller, 2002). The 12-week treatment program involved either DBT for 29 adolescents (mean age of 16.1 years) or a treatment-as-usual comparison group for 82 adolescents (mean age of 15 years). Those in the DBT group participated in DBT therapy through weekly individual therapy sessions and multifamily skills training sessions. The comparison group participated in weekly individual therapy and family therapy. Findings of this quasi-experimental study showed that the DBT group experienced a higher rate of treatment completion (62%) compared to the comparison group (40%). In addition, there were no psychiatric hospitalizations during treatment for participants in the DBT group while 13% of participants in the comparison group were hospitalized during treatment. Pre-post intervention analysis indicated that participants in the DBT group also experienced significant reductions in suicidal ideation and core aspects of borderline personality disorder (i.e., confusion about self, impulsivity, emotional dysregulation, and interpersonal difficulties). Participants also showed fewer psychiatric symptoms (e.g., anxiety and depression) following treatment. Pre-post intervention data were not collected for the comparison group (Rathus & Miller, 2002).

In another study, Canadian adolescents (14–17 years of age) largely from white ethnic groups participated in either DBT or treatment-as-usual in one of two psychiatric inpatient units involved in the study (Katz et al., 2004). One unit used a DBT approach while the second unit used an approach based on psychodynamic treatment. The adolescents were diagnosed with depression and had previous suicide attempts or suicidal ideation. The mean number of days in the hospital was 18 days for both groups.

Treatment for the 26 adolescents in the DBT group included receiving daily DBT skills training sessions. They also received individual therapy twice a week in order to facilitate the DBT skills. The inpatient unit used a DBT approach to provide structure and foster DBT skills and nurses were trained in DBT skills. The 26 adolescents in the comparison group participated in daily psychodynamic group therapy sessions and received individual psychodynamic therapy at least once a week. Participants also received psychiatric medication management as required by their individual circumstances. Data analysis indicated that both groups showed improvements in symptoms of depression and suicidal ideation and behavior after treatment and at the 1-year follow-up. However, those in the DBT group experienced fewer incidents on the unit during hospitalization when compared with the psychodynamic treatment group (Katz et al., 2004).

The DBT treatment approach also was provided for 10 adolescents (12–18 years of age) through outpatient therapy in a US university clinic for children and adolescents with bipolar disorder (Goldstein, Axelson, Birmaher, & Brent, 2007). Patients also were provided with psychiatric medication management during the study. The participants received 12 bi-weekly 60-minute individual sessions and 12 bi-weekly 60-minute family skills training sessions (provided to individual families) over the course of the first six months of treatment. Information and education about bipolar disorder in adolescents, and DBT for adolescents, also was included in initial sessions. Participants then received an additional six 60-minute individual sessions and six 60-minute family skills training sessions over the course of the second six months of treatment (to strengthen and practice skills learned in the first six-month period of treatment). Therapists provided skills coaching by telephone to participants and diary cards were used to monitor behavior and medication use. Parents and adolescents indicated a high level of treatment satisfaction and posttest analysis for the nine program completers showed reductions in suicidal behaviors, depressive symptoms, emotional dysregulation, and nonsuicidal self-injury (Goldstein, Axelson, Birmaher, & Brent, 2007).

The efficacy of DBT-A also was assessed in a pilot study conducted in a psychiatric outpatient setting in Germany. Twelve girls (aged 13–19 years) with BPD symptoms or a diagnosis of BPD with co-occurring suicidal behavior and/or nonsuicidal self-injurious behavior participated in the study (Fleischhaker et al., 2011). Treatment included weekly 60-minute individual therapy sessions and a weekly 2-hour multifamily skills training group. Therapy sessions continued for between 16 and 24 weeks depending upon the school holiday schedule. Consistent with DBT-A, participants and their parents learned and practiced skills in mindfulness, interpersonal effectiveness, distress tolerance, emotional regulation, and communication skills. Participants also were offered regular phone calls with their therapist as needed (Fleischhaker et al., 2011).

Nine of the 12 participants completed the program. Post-intervention findings indicated that criteria related to the diagnosis of BPD decreased in the participants following treatment, including suicidal ideation and non-suicidal self-injury. In addition, participants showed fewer symptoms of depression and decreased emotion dysregulation following the intervention (Fleischhaker et al., 2011).

In summary, programs based on DBT capitalize on cognitive-behavioral theory, developmental neuroscience, and positive psychology to help adolescents struggling with a variety of emotional challenges. Treatment completion and satisfaction levels indicated that these programs showed promise for helping adolescents experiencing serious mental health crises. These programs contributed to positive psychological benefits for participants including changes in emotional self-regulation (e.g., reductions in emotional dysregulation, anxiety and depression, suicidal ideation and suicidal behaviors, and nonsuicidal self-injury) as well as reductions in core aspects of BPD. In addition, outpatient DBT programs for adolescents have the potential to reduce or eliminate inpatient psychiatric hospitalizations during outpatient treatment. The following case example illustrates the application of DBT treatment for an adolescent struggling with behavioral and emotional challenges. This example shows how use of the DBT principles are used to bring about change and capitalize on strengths for young people.

Karen's Story

Karen is a 13-year-old child from a military family. Her parents, Shana and Ken, serve in the Army. Although originally from Trenton, New Jersey, the family has lived in many different places throughout their service. They recently moved from Alaska to Texas. Karen's mother had experienced two deployments and her father is currently on his second deployment.

Karen has attended many different schools and typically adjusted well in each new school. However, as Karen entered the 7th grade in her new school, she found herself experiencing anxiety that she had never experienced before. She missed her friends from Alaska and she worried about her father. She became withdrawn and incommunicative with her mother, teachers, and classmates.

Karen's mother, Shana, sought Karen out one day after school. She found Karen in her room and noticed that Karen had quickly pulled her shirt sleeve down over her wrist. Shana pulled the sleeve back and saw that Karen had purposefully cut herself. Karen admitted that she had cut herself with a small penknife. Karen also admitted that this was not the first time she had cut herself; she had many scars on her legs and arms. Karen's mother was frightened when she discovered the extent of the behavior and took Karen to be evaluated at her local emergency department. The emergency department psychiatric evaluator made a provisional diagnosis of major depressive disorder and arranged to have Karen admitted to the adolescent inpatient psychiatric unit in the hospital.

The unit uses a dialectical behavioral therapy (DBT) model for treating youth. Due to insurance limitations, the program is only two weeks in duration. The DBT program is adapted to address the brief treatment period. Youth participate in twice weekly individual therapy with a clinician (trained in the DBT model). The individual therapist also is available for support throughout the hospitalization. Youth also participate in a daily (Monday-Friday) group skills program facilitated by the unit psychologist. All medical personnel, including the psychiatric nurse practitioners, are trained in the DBT model and support the youth through use of the DBT principles. A psychiatrist manages the medication needs of the youth.

Karen attended all scheduled individual and group sessions. She formed a supportive relationship with her primary therapist and worked with her therapist to develop a plan to manage her emotions and develop coping skills to prevent recurrence of the self-injury behavior. She discussed her fears related to her parents' deployments and her recent difficulties stemming from the loss of friendships. Karen found the DBT skills of core mindfulness and distress tolerance skills to be particularly helpful to her. She also found the peer support in the group program to provide a sense of belongingness she had recently lost.

Shana attended the multifamily group meetings at the unit and learned more about how to engage in self-care and how to implement elements of the DBT model at home to meet Karen's needs. Ken was able to speak with Karen's primary therapist by phone in order to keep him informed of Karen's progress. Karen was discharged after 14 days with a plan to meet her needs at home. She was referred to a community psychiatrist for medication management. She also was referred to a therapist in the community who has been trained in DBT and who enjoys working with adolescents and their families. This therapist runs groups for adolescents so Karen can continue her group counseling. Shana was provided with names of family therapists if this should be something the family would like to pursue in the future.

Interventions Adapted from Acceptance and Commitment Therapy

Acceptance and commitment therapy (ACT) is a therapeutic approach originally developed for adults and emphasizes the importance of context and psychological flexibility in an effort to address a wide range of presenting concerns (Hayes, Strosahl, & Wilson, 2012). In a clinical sense, ACT helps people learn ways to modify thinking habits through a change in perspective (Hayes, Strosahl, & Wilson, 2012). This occurs through engaging in processes including mindfulness, acceptance, understanding the connection between thoughts and actions, engaging the observer self, identification of values, and committed action on those values. These processes facilitate psychological flexibility by reducing inflexible attention, compromising values, inaction, impulsivity, or avoidance, and attachment to self and thoughts. Modifications to the ACT programs have been made for use with adolescents and research in this area is emerging (Hayes, Boyd, & Sewell, 2011; Murrell, & Scherbarth, 2011; Wicksell, Melin, Lekander, & Olsson, 2009; Wicksell, Melin, & Olsson, 2007).

Acceptance and commitment therapy for teens assists young people to incorporate both pleasant and unpleasant private experiences into their experiences in a way that allows them to live a full life. The youth are encouraged to accept responsibility for controlling and bringing about change in their own behavior when possible. Treatment interventions involve exposure and behavioral activation to help the teens to live consistent with their own goals and values (Greco et al., 2008).

A pilot study conducted in a children's hospital pain treatment program in Sweden illustrated that outpatient treatment based on ACT principles was helpful for 14 adolescents (aged 13–20 years) with chronic and debilitating pain (Wicksell, Melin, & Olsson, 2007). Pain conditions included foot pain, abdominal pain, back pain, and headache. Traditionally, pain treatment involves an effort to reduce pain and distress. In contrast, the adolescent participants in this study engaged in a number of activities and exercises, consistent with ACT, to clarify values and increase psychological flexibility and acceptance. The intervention included pain education, values clarification, and goal setting. Also, adolescents were encouraged to move toward acceptance of some pain and discomfort consistent with personal values, and to engage in enjoyable behaviors even in the face of pain and discomfort. Participants were coached to increase acceptance and release control of behavior, feelings, and thoughts. The adolescents were seen individually for between 5–29 weekly sessions (mean of 14.4 sessions). Parents also were involved in the treatment process and participated in separate weekly sessions (0–10 sessions, mean of 2.4 sessions) with similar exercises as the adolescents. Parents also were taught to coach their child to help implement the new perspectives at home (Wicksell, Melin, & Olsson, 2007).

Analysis of pretest and posttest data showed that the treatment helped the adolescents in a number of ways. Improvements were noted in functional ability (i.e., taking part in daily activities), school attendance, and coping with pain. Participants also reported less intensity of pain and less interference with daily life due to pain. These improvements were retained at follow-up assessments conducted at 3-months and 6-months after the therapy ended (Wicksell et al., 2007).

Another study in the same children's hospital pain treatment program in Sweden evaluated the effectiveness of an outpatient intervention for adolescents diagnosed with pain syndromes (Wicksell, Melin, Lekander, & Olsson, 2009). Pain conditions included headache, neck and back pain, and widespread pain in the muscles. Participants included 32 adolescents (aged 10–18 years) who were randomly assigned to either the ACT condition or a treatment-as-usual comparison condition. Those in the comparison group learned about stress management and engaged in relaxation and imagery exercises. Participants in this group also received other treatments as needed (e.g., physical exercises, transcutaneous electrical nerve stimulation treatment, and water exercises). Participants also met for regular sessions with the physician to monitor medication, with a physiotherapist, and either a psychiatrist or psychologist. Each adolescent participated in an average of 10 sessions with these professionals (Wicksell, Melin, Lekander, & Olsson, 2009).

Those in the ACT condition participated in individual 60-minute weekly sessions with a psychologist and a total of one or two 90-minute sessions with the therapist and parents. Participants received between 7 and 20 sessions (including individual, parental, and follow-up sessions) (Wicksell et al., 2009). These ACT sessions involved activities and exercises of values clarification and promotion of psychological flexibility and acceptance. Findings showed that participants in both groups showed improvements in most outcomes. However, those in the ACT group experienced greater improvements in quality of life and in beliefs and attitudes about pain and functioning despite pain and fear of being injured again. This also was the case in the follow-up assessments (3.5 and 6.5 months) (Wicksell et al., 2009).

Another pilot study evaluated ACT compared with treatment-as-usual for 38 adolescents (aged 12–18 years) with depressive symptoms (Hayes, Boyd, & Sewell, 2011). Individual therapy sessions took place in an outpatient mental health setting in Australia and occurred over 13 months. Participants were randomly assigned either to the ACT treatment adapted for adolescents (n=22) or the manualized psychotherapy treatment with cognitive and behavioral elements including goal setting, problem-solving, and crisis management (n=16). Findings indicated that adolescents in both conditions showed improvements in global functioning at post-treatment. However, adolescents in the ACT condition, compared with those in the CBT group, showed greater improvements in depressive symptoms following treatment (e.g., reductions in emotional distress, negative self-evaluation, and physical complaints).

In summary, ACT, with modified cognitive-behavioral and acceptance aspects, offers a favorable intervention for adolescents facing challenges including painful medical conditions. Participants in these programs are likely to see improvements in quality of life, global functioning, and behavioral and emotional self-regulation. For example, benefits may include reductions in physical complaints, less intensity of pain, improvements in functional ability, and less interference with daily life due to pain, and fewer depressive symptoms and less emotional distress. Cognitive benefits include determination to function despite fear of being injured again and fewer instances of negative self-evaluation.

Summary

Professionals working in counseling, behavioral health, and medical settings serving adolescents are faced with helping adolescents and their families during health challenges and times of emotional crisis. Many treatments are offered to address these challenges and mindfulness-based interventions have been adapted to meet these needs. These programs present unique opportunities for adolescents and their parents to relieve physical, emotional, and cognitive distress.

These mindfulness-based programs have been adapted to provide effective programming for vulnerable adolescents and to meet the unique needs of adolescents and their parents. They offer a wide range of benefits in diverse settings (e.g., hospitals, substance abuse treatment centers, inpatient and outpatient centers, mental health and psychiatric centers) in various countries (e.g., Belgium, Canada, Germany, the Netherlands, Sweden, the US).

The studies examined in this chapter represent early efforts to identify helpful mindfulness-based practices. However, these studies offer a solid foundation to help counselors, nurses, physicians, psychologists, social workers, psychiatrists, and other professionals working with adolescents choose interventions that may help the youth and their families. Theoretical perspectives useful for guiding mindfulness-based practice in these settings include developmental neuroscience, cognitive-behavioral theory, systems and ecological perspectives, the transtheoretical model of change, and positive psychology.

Resources

	Books
Baer (2014)	*Mindfulness-based Treatment Approaches: Clinician's Guide to Evidence Base and Applications*
Biegel (2009)	*Mindfulness-based Stress Reduction for Teens*
Hayes, Strosahl, and Wilson (2012)	*Acceptance and Commitment Therapy: TheProcess and Practice of Mindful Change*
Linehan (2014)	*DBT Skills Training Manual*
Miller, Rathus, and DeBose (2007)	*Dialectical Behavior Therapy for Adolescents*
Rathus & Miller (2014)	*DBT® Skills Manual for Adolescents*
Semple & Lee (2014)	*Mindfulness-based Cognitive Therapy for Children*
Turrell & Bell (2016)	*ACT for Adolescents: Treating Teens and Adolescents in Individual and Group Therapy*
	Websites
Association for Contextual Behavioral Science-ACT information	https://contextualscience.org/act
Linehan Institute-DBT information	http://www.linehaninstitute.org/research.php
MBCT.com	http://mbct.com
Stressed Teens-MBSR-T information	http://www.stressedteens.com

References

Ames, C. S., Richardson, J., Payne, S., Smith, P., & Leigh, E. (2014). Mindfulness-based cognitive therapy for depression in adolescents. *Child and Adolescent Mental Health, 19*(1), 74–78. DOI:10.1111/camh.12034

Baer, R. A. (Ed.). (2014). *Mindfulness-based treatment approaches: Clinician's guide to evidence base and applications.* San Diego, CA: Academic Press.

Biegel, G. M. (2009). *Mindfulness-based stress reduction for teens: How you can use mindfulness to stop stressing.* Oakland, CA: New Harbinger.

Biegel, G. M., Brown, K. W., Shapiro, S. L, & Schubert, C. (2009). Mindfulness-based stress reduction for the treatment of adolescent psychiatric outpatients: A randomized clinical trial. *Journal of Clinical and Consulting Psychology, 77*(5), 855–866.

Bögels, S., Hoogstad, B., Van Dun, L., De Shutter, S., & Restifo, K. (2008). Mindfulness training for adolescents with externalising disorders and their parents. *Behavioural and Cognitive Psychotherapy, 36*(2), 193–209.

Bootzin, R. R., & Stevens, S. J. (2005). Adolescents, substance abuse, and the treatment of insomnia and daytime sleepiness. *Clinical Psychology Review, 25* (5), 629–644.

Cook, N. E., & Gorraiz, M. (2016). Dialectical behavior therapy for nonsuicidal self-injury and depression among adolescents: Preliminary meta-analytic evidence. *Child and Adolescent Mental Health, 21*(2), 81–89.

Deplus, S., Billieux, J., Scharff, C., & Philippot, P. (2016). A mindfulness-based group intervention for enhancing self-regulation of emotion in late childhood and adolescence: A pilot study. *International Journal of Mental Health and Addiction, 14*(5), 775–790.

Fleischhaker, C., Böhme, R., Sixt, B., Brück, C., Schneider, C., & Schulz, E. (2011). Dialectical behavioral therapy for adolescents (DBT-A): a clinical trial for patients with suicidal and self-injurious behavior and borderline symptoms with a one-year follow-up. *Child and Adolescent Psychiatry and Mental Health, 5*(1), 1–10.

Goldstein, T. R., Axelson, D. A., Birmaher, B., & Brent, D. A. (2007). Dialectical behavior therapy for adolescents with bipolar disorder: A 1-year open trial. *Journal of the American Academy of Child & Adolescent Psychiatry, 46*(7), 820–830.

Greco, L. A., Blomquist, K. K., Acra, S., & Moulton, D. (2008). Acceptance and commitment therapy for adolescents with functional abdominal pain: Results of a pilot investigation. *Unpublished Manuscript.*

Haydicky, J., Wiener, J., Badali, P., Milligan, K., & Ducharme, J. M. (2012). Evaluation of a mindfulness-based intervention for adolescents with learning disabilities and co-occurring ADHD and anxiety. *Mindfulness, 3*(2), 151–164.

Hayes, L., Boyd, C. P., & Sewell, J. (2011). Acceptance and commitment therapy for the treatment of adolescent depression: A pilot study in a psychiatric outpatient setting. *Mindfulness, 2*(2), 86–94.

Hayes, S. C., Strosahl, K. D., & Wilson, K. G. (2012). *Acceptance and commitment therapy: The process and practice of mindful change.* New York, NY: Guilford Press.

Kabat-Zinn J. (1990). *Full catastrophe living: Using the wisdom of your body and mind to face stress, pain and illness.* New York, NY: Delacorte.

Katz, L. Y., Cox, B. J., Gunasekara, S., & Miller, A. L. (2004). Feasibility of dialectical behavior therapy for suicidal adolescent inpatients. *Journal of the American Academy of Child & Adolescent Psychiatry, 43*(3), 276–282.

Linehan, M. M. (2014). *DBT skills training manual.* New York, NY: Guilford Publications.

Linehan, M. M., Armstrong, H. E., Suarez, A., Allmon, D., & Heard, H. L. (1991). Cognitive-behavioral treatment of chronically parasuicidal borderline patients. *Archives of General Psychiatry, 48*(12), 1060–1064.

MacPherson, H. A., Cheavens, J. S., & Fristad, M. A. (2013). Dialectical behavior therapy for adolescents: Theory, treatment adaptations, and empirical outcomes. *Clinical Child and Family Psychology Review, 16*(1), 59–80.

Miller, A.L., Rathus, J.H., & DeBose (2007). Dialectical behavior therapy for adolescents. In K. Keorner & L. DiMeff (Eds.) *Dialectical behavior therapy: Applications across disorders and settings* (pp. 245–263). New York, NY: Guilford Press.

Murrell, A. R., & Scherbarth, A. J. (2011). State of the research & literature address: ACT with children, adolescents and parents. *The International Journal of Behavioral Consultation and Therapy, 7*(1), 15–22.

Rathus, J. H., & Miller, A. L. (2002). Dialectical behavior therapy adapted for suicidal adolescents. *Suicide and Life-threatening Behavior, 32*(2), 146–157.

Rathus, J. H., & Miller, A. L. (2014). *DBT® Skills manual for adolescents.* New York, NY: Guilford Publications.

Segal, Z. V., Williams, J. M. G., & Teasdale, J. D. (2002). *Mindfulness-based cognitive therapy for depression: A new approach to relapse prevention.* New York, NY: Guilford Press.

Semple, R. J., & Lee, J. (2014). Mindfulness-based cognitive therapy for children. In R. Baer (Ed.), *Mindfulness-based treatment approaches: Clinician's guide to evidence base and applications* (pp. 161–187). San Francisco, CA: Academic Press.

Semple, R. J., Lee, J., Rosa, D., & Miller, L. F. (2010). A randomized trial of mindfulness-based cognitive therapy for children: Promoting mindful attention to enhance social-emotional resiliency in children. *Journal of Child and Family Studies, 19*(2), 218–229.

Sibinga, E. M., Kerrigan, D., Stewart, M., Johnson, K., Magyari, T., & Ellen, J. M. (2011). Mindfulness-based stress reduction for urban youth. *The Journal of Alternative and Complementary Medicine, 17*(3), 213–218.

Singh, N. N., Lancioni, G. E., Joy, S. D. S., Winton, A. S. W., Sabaawi, M., Wahler, R. G., … Singh, J. (2007). Adolescents with conduct disorder can be mindful of their aggressive behavior. *Journal of Emotional and Behavioral Disorders, 15*(1), 56–63. DOI:10.1177/10634266070150010601

Turrell, S. L., & Bell, M. (2016). *ACT for Adolescents: Treating teens and adolescents in individual and group therapy.* Oakland, CA: New Harbinger Publications.

Van De Weijer-Bergsma, E., Formsma, A. R., De Bruin, E. I., & Bögels, S. M. (2012). The effectiveness of mindfulness training on behavioral problems and attentional functioning in adolescents with ADHD. *Journal of Child and Family Studies, 21*(5), 775–787. DOI:10.1007/s10826-011-9531

Wicksell, R., Melin, L., Lekander, M., & Olsson, G. (2009). Evaluating the effectiveness of exposure and acceptance strategies to improve functioning and quality of life in longstanding pediatric pain: A randomized controlled trial. *Pain, 141*, 248–257.

Wicksell, R., Melin, L., & Olsson, G. (2007). Exposure and acceptance in the rehabilitation of adolescents with idiopathic chronic pain: A pilot study. *European Journal of Pain, 11*(3), 267–274.

Zoogman, S., Goldberg, S. B., Hoyt, W. T., & Miller, L. (2015). Mindfulness interventions with youth: A meta-analysis. *Mindfulness, 6*(2), 290–302.

CHAPTER 6

Home, Community-Based, and Specialized Settings

Introduction

Previous chapters have focused on mindfulness and meditation programs for adolescents in educational settings, and in counseling, behavioral health, and medical settings. There are times when it is appropriate to offer these programs in other settings such as home, community, or juvenile justice and correctional settings.

Teaching meditation practices in home settings allows individualized treatment for adolescents with unique and challenging conditions that result in behavioral problems including aggression. In contrast, The Center for Mind-Body Medicine's (CMBM) programs are offered in community settings in which adolescents have faced traumatic circumstances related to war or natural disasters. In addition, mindfulness and meditation programs are being introduced into residential, juvenile justice, and correctional settings to support adolescents and to help them cope with stressful circumstances common in these settings.

These innovative programs offer adolescents an opportunity to work toward improved health and wellness and provide skills to regulate behavior, thoughts, and emotions. Thus, this chapter examines the research emerging from mindfulness and meditation interventions for adolescents in home, community-based, and specialized settings. A case example illustrates the application of a mindfulness-based program for adolescents in a juvenile justice setting.

B.L. Wisner, *Mindfulness and Meditation for Adolescents*,
DOI 10.1057/978-1-349-95207-6_6

Home-Based Mindfulness Practice

Helping adolescents learn mindfulness or meditation practices in their own homes is a creative response to challenging behavioral circumstances. This is exemplified in the work of Nirbhay Singh and colleagues in their use of the Mindfulness-Based Intervention (MBI) called *Meditation on the Soles of the Feet* (Singh et al., 2007). This method has been used to help adolescents in outpatient therapy programs as described in Chapter 5 (Singh et al., 2007), but also has been used to help adolescents in home-based programs (Singh et al., 2011; Singh, Lancioni, Myers, Karazsia, Courtney, & Nugent, 2016). Multiple-baseline design studies showed that adolescents diagnosed with autism spectrum disorders (Singh et al., 2011) and adolescents with Prader-Willi syndrome (Singh et al., 2016) have found *Meditation on the Soles of the Feet* helpful.

Meditation on the Soles of the Feet

Meditation on the Soles of the Feet is a mindfulness practice that incorporates acceptance of emotions with self-regulation through redirection of attention to the sensations in the soles of the feet. Following individual instruction and guidance in the technique, adolescents are able to better regulate emotions and behaviors in emotionally challenging circumstances (Singh et al., 2007).

The *Meditation on the Soles of the Feet* intervention was used as a behavioral management skill to help three adolescent boys (aged 14, 16, and 17 years) with Autism Spectrum Disorder (Singh et al., 2011). Each participant's mother was trained in the meditation technique and was encouraged to use the technique in their own lives. The parents and siblings of the participants recorded episodes of aggression by the participants. Baseline periods varied by participant and lasted between three and ten weeks. Following the baseline period, the participant's mother taught their child the *Meditation on the Soles of the Feet* method by conducting daily 30-minute training sessions for 5 days. The adolescent was encouraged to breathe naturally, stay in the present moment, and learn to shift attention from uncomfortable emotions to the soles of the feet until a feeling of calmness was achieved. Adolescents were encouraged to practice the technique twice a day and to use the technique when emotionally challenging feelings, thoughts, or behaviors surfaced. Adolescents also had access to a recording modeling the intervention and were encouraged to periodically practice the technique (Singh et al., 2011).

Baseline figures indicated that the mean number of aggressive incidents ranged from 14–20 incidents per week for the three participants (Singh et al., 2011). The intervention phase varied by participant and lasted between 23 and 30 weeks; this phase was completed when the adolescent had not engaged in an episode of physical aggression for a one-month period. Thus, findings indicated that the mindfulness intervention was effective in reducing physical aggression in response to emotionally provoking experiences. Follow-up data were collected for a three-year period and indicated that significant reductions in aggressive behavior were sustained (Singh et al., 2011).

Another study using the *Meditation on the Soles of the Feet* method was conducted with adolescents diagnosed with Prader–Willi syndrome (PWS) (Singh et al., 2016). Prader–Willi syndrome is a genetic disorder with neurological and developmental concerns resulting in growth, intellectual development, and eating problems due to functioning of the thalamus (Cassidy, Schwartz, Miller, & Driscoll, 2012). Three boys, aged 16, 17, and 19 years of age participated in the study. All of the participants exhibited verbal and physical aggression, due to PWS, when restrictions were placed on food availability. Parents tracked the instances of aggression in all phases of the study (Singh et al., 2016).

The baseline period varied by participant (3–7 weeks) during which parents were trained in the meditation technique and were encouraged to use the technique in their own lives. Following the baseline period, both parents taught their child the *Meditation on the Soles of the Feet* method. During this five-day training period, the parents guided the child through the method and encouraged use of the technique to head off episodes of anger and aggression. Parents helped the child learn and practice the technique by first having them breathe naturally, imagine a time of anger, and then shift attention to the soles of the feet. This process was encouraged until a feeling of calmness was achieved. Adolescents also had access to a recording of a parent modeling the intervention and were encouraged to practice the technique at various times. During the intervention phase, daily practice of the method was encouraged and this phase lasted for between 33 and 37 weeks (varying by participant) (Singh et al., 2016).

Data were collected for a 12-month period and findings indicated that the mindfulness intervention was effective in reducing verbal aggression and eliminating physical aggression in response to emotionally provoking experiences. These improvements were maintained at the 12-month follow-up period (Singh et al., 2016).

In summary, it is likely that home-based mindfulness practices will play an important role in helping many adolescents with special needs to learn self-regulation skills. The *Meditation on the Soles of the Feet* practice provides a useful example of a simple and versatile skill that can be taught to parents who can then teach the practice to their children. The role of developmental neuroscience and the systems perspectives help us understand how this practice can support individual changes in physiological and emotional behavior in the context of the home and family. Psychological benefits of the practice include self-regulation as evidenced by reductions in verbal and physical aggression in response to emotionally provoking experiences.

Community-Based Meditation Programs

As mentioned in Chapter 1, James Gordon of the CMBM has pioneered a program with mindfulness and meditation components for those in communities exposed to war or natural disasters. These programs are offered in diverse settings across the globe. The CMBM's website offers examples of how these programs are being implemented in such locations as Gaza, Israel, Haiti, and Kosovo (https://cmbm.org). Research studies of CMBM programs in educational settings were described in Chapter 4. CMBM programs also are offered in community settings in which large segments of the population have been exposed to trauma due to natural disasters or political violence.

The Center for Mind-Body Medicine

The CMBM's program was offered in Gaza to 571 Palestinian children and adolescents exposed to political violence (Staples, Abdel Atti, & Gordon, 2011). The group programs were offered in community-based nongovernment organizations. A 10-session mind-body skills group program was offered in 2-hour sessions twice a week over the course of 5 weeks. Each group was comprised of 8–10 group members. Group topics included breath awareness exercises, meditation and movement activities, guided imagery, and autogenic training. Other activities included simple biofeedback exercises, exploration of the family constellation through diagramming, and creative writing and drawing exercises. Group support was promoted and participants were encouraged to share their experiences with each other (Staples, Abdel Atti, & Gordon, 2011).

A subset of 129 children and adolescents (8–18 years of age) with posttraumatic stress disorder (PTSD) were identified from the larger group of participants. Data analysis indicated reductions in symptoms of PTSD, depression, and hopelessness for participants following the mind-body skills groups. Even in the face of continued political upheaval and economic challenges, many of these improvements were maintained at the 7-month follow-up (Staples, Abdel Atti, & Gordon, 2011).

This research illustrates the way in which the CMBM mind-body skills group program helps young people exposed to war and trauma. Elements of cognitive-behavioral theory, systems and ecological perspectives, and the Transtheoretical Model of Change may be found in the CMBM's mind-body skills programs. The psychological benefits of this program include reductions in symptoms of PTSD, depression, and hopelessness. These are essential elements in the healing process and provide a means of empowerment for those harmed by community-based marginalization, discrimination, and violence.

Use of Mindfulness and Meditation in Specialized Settings

Adolescents are learning to understand themselves, to connect with others, and to regulate behaviors and emotions. During the course of an adolescent's developmental trajectory, there may be times when the adolescent experiences a disruption in these processes that results in a placement out of the home. Adolescents may find themselves in a variety of placement settings including residential treatment centers, homeless shelters, or correctional settings. In these programs and settings, adolescents may be offered a number of activities and interventions to help them cope with personal circumstances or placement challenges. These interventions may include mindfulness or meditation practices or programs offered as an aspect of programming. While there is scant literature in this area, there are some examples that help to illustrate use of these programs to support the health and well-being of adolescents in these settings.

Residential Settings

Residential treatment centers and wilderness therapy programs for adolescents involve placement out of the home with comprehensive care that addresses emotional and physical health needs (Bettmann & Jasperson, 2009). Meditation practices may be used in these settings as one aspect of the treatment program. For example, yoga has been used in residential treatment programming for traumatized youth (Spinazzola, Rhodes, Emerson, Earle, & Monroe, 2011), and mindfulness, meditation, and yoga practices have been integrated into wilderness therapy programs (Bettmann, Russel, & Parry, 2013).

Spinazzola et al. (2011) described a trauma-informed yoga program designed for use in residential settings. Although this program has not been the subject of research to date, it provides an interesting example of the potential of such practices to help youth in residential settings. The program is intended to serve youth 12–21 years of age who are experiencing serious emotional and behavioral problems as a result of previous trauma (e.g., suffering the suicide of a parent or severe neglect or abuse). Youth are invited to participate in optional yoga classes as appropriate given the adolescent's needs and therapeutic goals. Staff members also are invited to participate in yoga classes along with adolescent residents. Program exercises included breathing, mindfulness, and yoga practices that helped adolescents improve self-reflection and self-awareness of their bodies and emotions. The authors presented case vignettes illustrating how yoga may be particularly helpful for supporting self-regulation for the youth (Spinazzola et al., 2011).

As mentioned, mindfulness, meditation, and yoga practices also have been integrated into wilderness therapy programs. Bettmann et al. (2013) described an 8-week substance abuse recovery program for adolescents. Although the intervention is not considered an MBI, practices related to mindfulness, meditation, and yoga were integrated into the program in order to facilitate coping skills, self-awareness, and emotion regulation.

Data from 41 adolescents who had participated in the wilderness therapy program were analyzed. Findings indicated that program participants showed reductions in mental health symptoms including physical distress, suicidality, and eating disorders. Assessment of stage of change indicated that youth who originally lacked motivation to change as they entered the program moved from pre-contemplation, to action, and then to maintenance stages of change as treatment progressed (Bettmann et al., 2013). The study illustrated how incorporation of mindfulness, meditation, and yoga may support treatment in a wilderness setting.

Homeless Shelters

Youth experiencing homelessness are particularly vulnerable to emotional distress due to uncertain life circumstances. Programs are offered to help youth cope with these stressful events. For example, a spirituality development class with a mindfulness component was offered to 71 homeless youth in an urban shelter in the US (Grabbe, Nguy, & Higgins, 2012). The class was a modified version of the Yale University Spiritual Self-Schema program. The program was offered in 8 sessions over the course of 4 weeks and included breath awareness, skill development, and cognitive techniques. Content also encouraged alternative responses to habitual behaviors related to drug use, social behavior, and self-harm. In addition, use of mindfulness meditation skills, empathy, and compassion was encouraged to promote spiritual strengths (Grabbe, Nguy, & Higgins, 2012).

Thirty-nine of the youth (ages 17–23 years) completed at least four sessions of the class (Grabbe, Nguy, & Higgins, 2012), and posttest analysis showed increased resilience, increased spirituality (i.e., a greater sense of peace and meaning), a stronger sense of mental well-being, and a decrease in psychological symptoms (including emotional distress, depression, and anxiety) for participants who completed at least four class sessions. Qualitative analysis showed that youth who completed the program found the meditation to be particularly helpful and that the program helped them to improve their level of focus and to manage anger (Grabbe, Nguy, & Higgins, 2012).

Juvenile Justice Programs and Correctional Programs

Meditation programs also are used in institutional settings such as correctional settings. These programs offer a unique way for incarcerated youth to manage their own behavior and stress levels. For example, an MBI program for incarcerated youth has been developed by the Mind Body Awareness Project (MBA), a San Francisco Bay Area nonprofit organization (http://www.mbaproject.org). The MBA program is delivered in 10 weekly sessions with module topics designed to meet the specific needs of high-risk youth (http://www.mbaproject.org/about-mindfulness-3/our-curricula/). These topics are mindfulness, basic goodness, impulse regulation, emotional awareness, emotional intelligence, interpersonal relationships, empathy, forgiveness, negative core beliefs, and cause and effect. The 60-minute sessions include formal sitting mindfulness meditation (based on the Vipassana tradition) offered in a group setting with experiential activities (e.g. forgiveness meditation) and discussion topics (e.g., impulse regulation, empathy, and transforming negative core beliefs) (Himelstein, Hastings, Shapiro, & Heery, 2012b). Related resources for those working with this population include the book, *A mindfulness-based approach to working with high-risk adolescents* (Himelstein, 2013).

Elements of the MBA program (promoting self-awareness) were integrated with a drug education component to create an 8-week mindfulness-based substance abuse intervention program. This program was offered to 60 youth (aged 15–18 years) in a juvenile detention camp in the US (Himelstein, 2011). Drug education was integrated with formal and informal mindfulness practices, experiential exercises, and group discussions and was delivered in weekly 90-minute sessions. Six cohorts of 8–12 youth participated in the program over the course of 7 months. Qualitative results showed that participants were receptive to the program and to the delivery of drug use education. Youth also were appreciative of the approach of the program facilitators. Pre-posttest data analysis indicated that the 48 youth who completed the program experienced increased perceived risk of drug use and decreased impulsivity (Himelstein, 2011).

Himelstein, Hastings, Shapiro, and Heery (2012a) described outcomes of a qualitative study of the MBA program for incarcerated youth. The 23 boys (14–18 years of age) were incarcerated in a juvenile facility in the US. The program, with both formal and informal mindfulness meditation activities, was delivered in 10 weekly 60-minute sessions. Once the program concluded, participants were interviewed and digital recordings of the interviews provided the source of the data. Data analysis yielded five major themes related to the benefits of the MBI: increase in subjective well-being (e.g., relaxation and stress reduction), increase in self-regulation (e.g., emotional and behavioral), increase in self-awareness (e.g., self-contemplation and emotional awareness), group experiences (e.g., expression), and acceptance of the MBI (e.g., keeping an open mind about the program) (Himelstein et al., 2012a). In another aspect of the same study for incarcerated youth, quantitative analysis of pre-post-intervention data from 32 youth showed that self-reported perceived stress decreased and self-regulation increased after participation in the program (Himelstein, Hastings, Shapiro, & Heery, 2012b).

There is now a handbook describing the 12-session curriculum for a mindfulness-based substance abuse treatment for adolescents (Himelstein & Saul, 2015). This curriculum integrates practices from mindfulness, psychotherapy, and addiction treatment to formulate a Mindfulness-Based Substance Abuse

Treatment (MBSAT) program. While the group program was originally created for use in correctional settings, it also may be used in schools, clinics, inpatient and outpatient settings, and in community-based programs. The curriculum incorporates mindfulness meditation, mindfulness activities, mindfulness-based concepts, and substance abuse education with strategies for relapse prevention and promotion of a systemic outlook to substance use. The program includes topics related to mindfulness, reacting and responding, substance use, emotional awareness, neuro-development, cravings, triggers, family system, peers, and the external environment. The handbook offers a comprehensive overview of all sessions in the curriculum with a list of materials needed, learning objectives, session agenda, session summary, talking points, and sample scripts of meditation practices for facilitators. Also included in the handbook is information for educational topics and handouts and worksheets to use throughout the program (Himelstein & Saul, 2015). In support of cultural competence, Himelstein and Saul (2015) recommend adapting the program to meet the needs of adolescents from various backgrounds. For instance, when facilitators are working primarily with youth from underprivileged neighborhoods or ethnic groups different from their own, Himelstein and Saul recommend caution so that youth are not exposed to unsuitable cultural experiences. Himelstein and Saul recommend that facilitators review Kivel's (2011) ideas on ways to promote social justice and social responsibility while avoiding perpetuation of racism and oppression.

Other authors have investigated the benefits of mindfulness training combined with cognitive behavioral therapy (CBT) for youth incarcerated in an urban setting in the US (Leonard et al. 2013). Leonard et al. (2013) suggested that this type of program may ameliorate the heightened stress and potential negative effects on attention, emotion, and behavior experienced by youth incarcerated in a secure correctional facility. Incarcerated youth, aged 16–18 years and from primarily black and Latino ethnic groups, were randomly assigned (by dormitory) to the MBI intervention (n=147) or to a control intervention (n=117). Those in the MBI group engaged in formal mindfulness practices, CBT exercises, and reading assignments, and were encouraged to practice meditation outside of sessions. Those in the control group participated in a group program emphasizing awareness of attitudes and beliefs related to violence and substance use. Each of the interventions was offered in approximately 75-minute sessions for 3 to 5 weeks depending upon the needs of the facility. As expected, performance on attention tasks, for all participants, deteriorated over time (ostensibly due to the heightened stress of incarceration).

However, participants in the MBI group showed less deterioration in attentional tasks when compared with the control group. In addition, for those in the MBI group who practiced mindfulness outside of the group sessions, performance degradation remained stable over time rather than showing increased degradation over time (Leonard et al., 2013).

Barnert, Himelstein, Herbert, Garcia-Romeu, & Chamberlain (2014) described a program offered to 29 adolescent males (aged 14–18 years and primarily identifying as Latino) in a juvenile correctional facility. The program was based on the Mind Body Awareness Project's program for youth in juvenile justice facilities. There were four cohorts of US adolescents involved in the study. Two groups participated in a one-day meditation retreat plus a 10-week meditation program. The 7-hour retreat aspect of the program was conducted at a facility outside of the correctional center. Two groups participated in the 10-week meditation program without the one-day meditation retreat. For all groups, weekly 90-minute sessions included meditation practice and group discussion. Exercises included mindfulness of breathing, walking, eating, and the body scan. Participants were coached in nonjudgmental awareness and promotion of trust and emotional disclosure occurred through group activities and rituals (Barnert et al., 2014).

Analysis of data from this mixed-methods study showed the benefits of participation in the program. Posttest analyses indicated that participants exhibited enhanced self-regulation. No significant differences were reported between participants in the retreat plus the weekly sessions condition and the participants in the condition without the retreat (Barnert et al., 2014). Focus group data, related to participation in both the weekly session and the retreat, yielded six themes indicating benefits or challenges for the youth. Benefits included increased ability to manage emotions and behaviors, enhanced well-being, increased social cohesiveness, expanded self-awareness, and intention to continue the meditation practice. Some participants did not find meditation helpful or felt a resistance to sitting meditation or aspects of meditation such as keeping the eyes closed (Barnert et al., 2014).

This literature demonstrates the promise that mindfulness programs have for helping adolescents in residential centers, homeless shelters, and juvenile justice and correctional programs. Concepts from developmental neuroscience, cognitive-behavioral theory, systems and ecological perspectives, the transtheoretical model of change, and positive youth development help us understand how mindfulness and meditation practices can support adolescents in choosing how and when to make changes in their physiological, psychological, and social behavior.

These programs were well-received by many of the adolescents and research has demonstrated numerous benefits of the mindfulness and meditation programs offered in these settings. In particular, psychological benefits were frequent outcomes of the programs. For example, improvements in focus, coping skills, self-awareness, and emotion regulation (including anger management) were found. In addition, increased self-awareness, self-regulation and resilience, a stronger sense of mental well-being, and increased subjective well-being are potential outcomes of these programs. Other findings included decreased physical and emotional distress, depression, anxiety, stress, impulsivity, and suicidality. Programs with a mindfulness component also may help adolescents increase spiritual development and social cohesiveness and to move through stages of change as treatment progresses.

These findings represent great hope for helping youth marginalized and forgotten by many in society. Youth in these settings may feel frightened, disempowered, and hostile. Mindfulness and meditation programs represent concrete tools and exercises to employ as methods to help adolescents cope with these feelings and to promote decision-making informed by a balanced approach as the present moment is experienced and plans for the future are made. The following case example illustrates how an adolescent may benefit from an MBI developed for youth in juvenile justice settings.

Michael's Story

Michael is a 17-year-old living in New York City. He is an only child being raised by his mother, Caroline. Michael repeated two grades so he is in the tenth grade, while most of his friends are seniors. He has little in common with the younger students in his classes and often skips school. When he is in school he acts bored and ignores his teachers' directions. Michael is on probation after being charged with truancy and shoplifting in a local store.

When Michael was ten years old, Caroline was in a car accident and she sustained neurological damage when her head hit the windshield. Caroline has found it difficult to provide discipline for Michael and he often acts as her caretaker. Over the years, Michael has taken on more responsibility at home. He helps his mother with household chores and her medical appointments. Michael also does odd jobs in the neighborhood to bring home some money to contribute to the grocery shopping.

Recently, Michael and a few of his friends had been hanging out together after school; they were congregating in an abandoned house in their neighborhood where they drank beer and smoked marijuana. One evening the teens began breaking windows in the house and a neighbor called the authorities to report suspicious activity. Responding officers found Michael and his friends in the house; the boys were drunk and high. Michael was arrested, and because of his previous truancy and shoplifting offenses, he was placed in a juvenile detention center pending a court appearance.

Michael has been compliant with the center's programs and participates in structured activities during the day. However, evenings are difficult for Michael as he is consumed with worry about his mother. He feels a deep sense of sadness and guilt that alternates with intense anger. The center's counselor has worked with him to address these concerns and she has reached out to his mother to assess her ability to parent Michael. Michael's counselor suggested that he enroll in a new mindfulness substance abuse program that is offered at the center in the evenings. Michael agreed to participate because he thought this would "look good" for him when he appears in court.

Michael participated in the 4-week mindfulness substance abuse group program with nine other youth. The group leaders were experienced mindfulness practitioners with expertise leading group programs for youth. They provided rules and expectations for the youth and promoted group cohesion. The group met twice a week for an hour. Sessions included discussions of drug and alcohol use and abuse, the influence of family, peers, and school, and the development of new coping skills. The youth also learned about mindfulness and awareness, and practiced various mindfulness exercises. Michael, during the initial mindfulness practices, found it very difficult to stay in the moment because his thoughts continued to be consumed with his changing emotions. In addition, he was initially very quiet in the sessions and found it hard to engage in the discussions because he did not trust the other members. The group leaders understood that members may need time to adjust to the group process and they allowed Michael to move at his own pace.

During the third session, Michael told the members about his mother and how much he worries about her and how he feels he has let her down. The group leaders and the youth acknowledged Michael's awareness of his feelings and his concern for his mother. They encouraged Michael in his efforts to participate in the mindfulness exercises and offered tips for maintaining mindful awareness. Michael worked toward observing his thoughts and emotions with acceptance and non-judgment. Michael also learned about the effects of substance use, the connection between use and his emotions, and alternative ways to cope with stressful events and emotions.

As the sessions continued, Michael became a full participant in the group. He particularly enjoyed mindful walking and found that it helped him to stay in the moment. He successfully completed the mindfulness substance abuse group program.

Michael continues to struggle with his fears and feelings of anger and guilt as he waits for his court date. He works toward acceptance, non-judgment, and self-compassion as he acknowledges his emotions. He discusses this in individual sessions with the center's counselor and continues to work toward incorporating new coping skills into his life.

Summary

There are times when an adolescent is unable to control personal behavior at home. Mindfulness and meditation practices have the potential to help the adolescent learn new coping skills for behavioral and emotional regulation. In addition, societies have an obligation to provide for adolescents living in community, residential, and juvenile justice facilities. These youths require a broad range of supportive services and mindfulness and meditation programs offer options for providing coping skills and treatment options to adolescents in these circumstances. The interventions discussed in this chapter are designed to treat unresolved responses to traumatic events and to help adolescents reduce stress and regulate emotions and behaviors.

The literature on these interventions and programs provides a foundation for understanding the role that mindfulness and meditation practices and programs may play in homes and in treatment programs. Parents may play a pivotal role in teaching and supporting these practices in the home while counselors, psychologists, social workers, and other professionals play a key role in program planning and delivery of mindfulness and meditation interventions. Selected resources, including books and websites, are included at this end of this chapter. These resources may guide those wishing to incorporate programs in these settings.

The research on these interventions and programs provide helpful examples of successful mindfulness and meditation practices and programs in home, community, residential, and juvenile justice facilities. Given the scarcity of mindfulness and meditation programs in these settings, there is much work to be done to support adolescents who are often marginalized and forgotten.

Resources

	Books
Crichlow and Joseph (Eds.) (2015)	*Alternative Offender Rehabilitation and Social Justice: Arts and Physical Engagement in Criminal Justice and Community Settings*
Gordon (1996)	*Manifesto for a New Medicine: Your Guide to Healing Partnerships and the Wise use of Alternative Therapies.*
Himelstein (2013)	*A Mindfulness-based Approach to Working with High-risk Adolescents*
Himelstein and Saul (2015)	*Mindfulness-based Substance Abuse Treatment for Adolescents: A 12-session Curriculum*
	Websites
American Health and Wellness Institute (information on Soles of the Feet exercise)	https://www.ahwinstitute.com/our-services/community-and-organizational-training/soles-of-the-feet
The Center for Mind-Body Medicine	https://cmbm.org
David Lynch Foundation	https://www.davidlynchfoundation.org/prisons.html
The Mind Body Awareness Project	http://www.mbaproject.org
The Mindfulness Initiative	http://www.themindfulnessinitiative.org.uk
Prison Mindfulness Institute	http://www.prisonmindfulness.org

References

Barnert, E. S., Himelstein, S., Herbert, S., Garcia-Romeu, A., & Chamberlain, L. J. (2014). Exploring an intensive meditation intervention for incarcerated youth. *Child and Adolescent Mental Health*, *19*(1), 69–73.

Bettmann, J. E., & Jasperson, R. A. (2009, August). Adolescents in residential and inpatient treatment: A review of the outcome literature. In *Child & Youth Care Forum*, 38(4), 161–183.

Bettmann, J. E., Russell, K. C., & Parry, K. J. (2013). How substance abuse recovery skills, readiness to change and symptom reduction impact change processes in wilderness therapy participants. *Journal of Child and Family Studies, 22*(8), 1039–1050.

Cassidy, S. B., Schwartz, S., Miller, J. L., & Driscoll, D. J. (2012). Prader-Willi syndrome. *Genetics in Medicine, 14*(1), 10–26.

Crichlow, W., & Joseph, J. (Eds.). (2015). *Alternative Offender Rehabilitation and Social Justice: Arts and Physical Engagement in Criminal Justice and Community Settings.* New York, NY: Palgrave.

Gordon, J. S. (1996). *Manifesto for a new medicine: Your guide to healing partnerships and the wise use of alternative therapies.* Chicago, IL: Da Capo Press.

Grabbe, L., Nguy, S. T., & Higgins, M. K. (2012). Spirituality development for homeless youth: A mindfulness meditation feasibility pilot. *Journal of Child and Family Studies, 21*(6), 925–937.

Himelstein, S. (2011). Mindfulness-based substance abuse treatment for incarcerated youth: A mixed methods pilot study. *International Journal of Transpersonal Studies, 30*(1–2), 1–10.

Himelstein, S. (2013). *A mindfulness-based approach to working with high-risk adolescents.* New York, NY: Routledge.

Himelstein, S., Hastings, A., Shapiro, S., & Heery, M. (2012a). A qualitative investigation of the experience of a mindfulness-based intervention with incarcerated adolescents. *Child and Adolescent Mental Health, 17*(4), 231–237.

Himelstein, S., Hastings, A., Shapiro, S., & Heery, M. (2012b). Mindfulness training for self-regulation and stress with incarcerated youth: A pilot study. *Probation Journal, 59*(2), 151–165.

Himelstein, S., & Saul, S. (2015). *Mindfulness-based substance abuse treatment for adolescents: A 12-session curriculum.* New York, NY: Routledge.

Kivel, P. (2011). *Uprooting Racism: How White People Can Work for Racial Justice* (3rd *Edition).* Gabriola Island, Canada: New Society Publishers.

Leonard, N. R., Jha, A. P., Casarjian, B., Goolsarran, M., Garcia, C., Cleland, C. M., & Massey, Z. (2013). Mindfulness training improves attentional task performance in incarcerated youth: A group randomized controlled intervention trial. *Frontiers in Psychology, 4*(792), 1–10.

Singh, N. N., Lancioni, G. E., Joy, S. D. S., Winton, A. S. W., Sabaawi, M., Wahler, R. G., ... Singh, J. (2007). Adolescents with conduct disorder can be mindful of their aggressive behavior. *Journal of Emotional and Behavioral Disorders, 15*, 56–63. DOI:10.1177/10634266070150010601

Singh, N. N., Lancioni, G. E., Manikam, R., Winton, A. S. W., Singh, A. N. A., Singh, J., ... Singh, A. D. A. (2011). A mindfulness-based strategy for selfmanagement of aggressive behavior in adolescents with autism. *Research in Autism Spectrum Disorders, 5*, 1153–1158. DOI:10.1016/j.rasd.2010.12.012

Singh, N. N., Lancioni, G. E., Myers, R. E., Karazsia, B. T., Courtney, T. M., & Nugent, K. (2016). A mindfulness-based intervention for selfmanagement of verbal and physical aggression by adolescents with Prader–Willi syndrome. *Developmental Neurorehabilitation*, 1–8. DOI:10.3109/17518423.2016.1141436

Spinazzola, J., Rhodes, A. M., Emerson, D., Earle, E., & Monroe, K. (2011). Application of yoga in residential treatment of traumatized youth. *Journal of the American Psychiatric Nurses Association, 17*(6), 431–444.

Staples, J. K., Abdel Atti, J. A., & Gordon, J. S. (2011). Mind-body skills groups for posttraumatic stress disorder and depression symptoms in Palestinian children and adolescents in Gaza. *International Journal of Stress Management, 18*(3), 246–262.

CHAPTER 7

Recommendations, Conclusions, and Future Directions

Introduction

The literature on the benefits of mindfulness and meditation practices and programs for adolescents is growing. Although this literature is only a small portion of the broader literature base about mindfulness and meditation programs, the importance of these practices and programs for adolescents may be established from the emerging literature base. The evidence-based practice and practice-based evidence is expanding quickly and these programs will be increasingly offered in diverse settings. A review of the current literature, as presented in previous chapters, shows that these practices and programs have many benefits.

The central benefits of mindfulness and meditation programming for adolescents are reviewed in this chapter and this provides the foundation for offering ideas for those interested in program development. In order to provide the best programs for adolescents, it is imperative that these activities and interventions be grounded in theory appropriate to adolescent development in a contemporary context. Ideas also are presented so that those interested in teaching mindfulness and meditation to adolescents, or those incorporating mindfulness into diverse settings, may do so in an informed manner. Innovative program options and future directions for mindfulness and meditation programming for adolescents also are addressed in this chapter along with cultural and global considerations related to this programming.

B.L. Wisner, *Mindfulness and Meditation for Adolescents*,
DOI 10.1057/978-1-349-95207-6_7

The Central Benefits of Mindfulness and Meditation for Adolescents

Adolescence is a time of life that brings with it personal growth opportunities and personal risks. As such, offering innovative interventions and practices to adolecents may facilitate development, reduce risks, and support resiliency. Mindfulness and meditation practices for adolescents are varied and increasingly the subject of research studies. Thus, a broad range of studies supporting the benefits of mindfulness and meditation programs are available in the literature. These benefits include physiological changes, emotional flexibility, and emotional and behavioral regulation. For example, increases in cardiovascular health, reduction of stress, and increased wellness, self-awareness, self-esteem, and trust in self and others have been found for adolescents participating in diverse programs. In addition, improvements in relationships occur and spiritual and identity development are fostered when adolescents participate in mindfulness and meditation programs. Thus, as illustrated in Chapter 3, these benefits encompass biological, psychological, social, and cultural contexts (Black, 2015; Felver, Celis-de Hoyos, Tezanos, & Singh, 2016; Zenner, Herrnleben-Kurz, & Walach, 2014; Zoogman, Goldberg, Hoyt, & Miller, 2015).

These benefits have been demonstrated for mindfulness and meditation techniques and programs across a variety of settings and in diverse geographical locations. The usefulness of mindfulness and meditation programs serving adolescents in educational, counseling, behavioral health, hospitals, psychiatric centers, and juvenile justice facilities has been demonstrated. These benefits are seen in many geographical locations across the globe (e.g., Belgium, Canada, Germany, the Netherlands, Sweden, the US). In addition, home-based mindfulness practices also have been helpful for adolescents and their families coping with diverse medical, behavioral, and psychological conditions (Black, 2015; Felver, Celis-de Hoyos, Tezanos, & Singh, 2016; Zenner, Herrnleben-Kurz, & Walach, 2014; Zoogman, Goldberg, Hoyt, & Miller, 2015).

Thus, it is clear that mindfulness and meditation programs offer options for supporting adolescents in diverse settings. Professionals in these settings, including teachers, counselors, psychologists, nurses, psychiatrists, and social workers, are encouraged to investigate potential options for using these interventions to help adolescents. As we also have seen, there are practices that parents can learn and teach to their children. This shows the flexibility and adaptability of these practices. The case examples in this book provided ideas for implementing mindfulness and meditation programs for adolescents who face a number of challenges and require treatment for these concerns.

Connecting Theory, Research, and Practice for Optimal Outcomes

Understanding the historical, developmental, and systemic factors important in adolescent development is helpful when developing interventions for youth. Since there are a growing number of mindfulness and meditation programs, it is important that those responsible for offering these programs for youth understand relevant theoretical foundations underlying both adolescent development and mindfulness and meditation practices.

These theories include developmental neuroscience, cognitive-behavioral theory, the systems and ecological perspectives, the transtheoretical model of change, identity development, and positive youth development. By incorporating these theories and perspectives into program development, the quality of mindfulness and meditation programs is enhanced. In order to provide competent and ethical mindfulness and meditation practices and programming for adolescents, it also is necessary to integrate knowledge of relevant theory with research findings, and to address practice skills. In addition, theories of meditation contribute to understanding how mindfulness and meditation bring about outcomes for adolescents. A comprehensive overview of these theories is discusssed in Chapter 2.

Developmental neuroscience provides a foundation for understanding how mindfulness and meditation contribute to neurological and physiological changes for adolescents. One example of this is related to impulsivity and risk-taking behaviors. When adolescents are able to control attention and regulate their emotions they are less likely to be impulsive and to engage in risky behaviors (Sanger & Dorjee, 2015). Thus, mindfulness and meditation programs can be developed with an understanding of typical neurological development. Furthermore, the effects of mindfulness and meditation practices on thinking and action is illuminated by cognitive-behavioral theory. There are practices that allow observation of thoughts and behaviors and in so doing, promote an understanding of how the mind works.

In a religious sense, mindfulness and meditation may be practiced with no goal in mind or as a vehicle for spiritual development. In contrast, the practices and programs discussed in this book are largely secular in nature and are typically used with a goal in mind. Cognitive-behavioral theory is particularly relevant to these practices as are the cognitive-directed methods of meditation (e.g., mindfulness and Tai Chi Chuan) as described by Nash and Newberg (2013). Goals of mindfulness and meditation practices often are related to helping adolescents overcome difficult circumstances or challenges (i.e., stress, anxiety, posttraumatic stress disorder, attention deficit hyperactivity disorder). However, using principles from positive youth development, mindfulness and meditation programming also may be used to promote strengths in adolescents.

Systems and ecological theories provide a foundation for understanding adolescent development within family, school, neighborhood, and cultural contexts. In addition, understanding the process of adolescent identity development contributes to understanding why some adolescents will be more attracted to mindfulness and meditation practices than others. Along with identity development, the transtheoretical model of change may be used to gauge when mindfulness and meditation practices may be particularly helpful for adolescents.

As demonstrated in Chapter 3, the research on mindfulness and meditation practices and programs with adolescents is still in its infancy. A synthesis of these findings is presented in a subsequent section of this chapter. By using knowledge of theory, and accessing research guided by theory, professionals working with adolescents are positioned to make informed choices about mindfulness and meditation programming.

Mindfulness and Meditation Program Development for Adolescents

Crucial decisions face those interested in developing and teaching mindfulness and meditation practices and programs for adolescents. It is incumbent upon program developers, teachers, and clinicians to be informed by best practices and recommendations mentioned in the literature. Decisions must be made about the setting for the intervention, the type of intervention or practice used, who will teach or provide the practice, and an appropriate dosage (i.e., the frequency and duration of the practice and program). The setting will often determine many of the decisions made about the program or practice.

Program Setting

Settings for mindfulness and meditation programs include schools, clinics, hospitals, residential settings, communities, juvenile justice centers, and homes. It is important that interventions offered in diverse settings be chosen with the needs of the youth in mind. For example, the literature shows that mindfulness and meditation programs are becoming more common in educational settings. These settings offer access to many adolescents in a setting in which they spend much of their time. Incorporating programs into these settings makes sense and offers important opportunities to reach many adolescents. Meiklejohn et al. (2012) stressed the importance of an inclusive perspective in which the needs of both students and teachers are considered when developing mindfulness programs. Hence, programming is better supported when school-based professionals (i.e., teachers, administrators, psychologists, nurses, counselors, and social workers) collaborate to offer programming for students.

While mindfulness and meditation programs are frequently used to help adolescents, certain challenges may face program developers. For example, time constraints may be faced and setting aside time for a meditation program is often difficult. Monitoring recommended home-based meditation practice is challenging. In addition, while this is rare, parents may object to the program. These challenges are not insurmountable; parents may be better informed and educated about practices, programming may be offered in brief time periods, practices may be used that adolescents can easily integrate into home settings, and recorded sessions may be provided for home practice (Deplus, Billieux, Scharff & Philippot, 2016; Sibinga, Kerrigan, Stewart, Johnson, Magyari, & Ellen, 2011; Singh et al., 2011).

Mindfulness and meditation interventions offered in specialized settings also will necessitate careful planning for potential challenges. For example, those offering programs in juvenile justice centers will need to work closely with administration and correctional staff so that the program and participants will be supported. Time constraints will likely be encountered and the program will need to fit within the limitations of the regular schedule of activities. Youth may be unable to complete the program due to infractions unrelated to the program or due to early dismissal from the center (Himelstein, Hastings, Shapiro, & Heery, 2012).

Environmental and scheduling challenges also may be encountered when offering mindfulness and meditation programs, including physical setting limitations and timing of programs. Providing a relatively hospitable environment for meditation is important, but not always possible. Rooms that are noisy, too warm, or too cold may present challenges. Likewise, programming offered at certain times of the day may present challenges for adolescent participants (e.g., early in the morning or after lunch). Rooms that are cramped may not allow for movement exercises such as yoga or walking meditation (Himelstein et al., 2012; Wisner, 2013). Some of these challenges may be addressed during the planning process while other challenges may be unavoidable.

A variety of mindfulness and meditation practices are currently used with adolescents. The type of practice chosen will depend upon the particular adolescent population served, the setting, and the reason for providing a practice or intervention.

Type of Intervention or Practice

Previous chapters addressed information on diverse mindfulness and meditation practices and programs including mindfulness-based interventions (MBIs), Transcendental Meditation (TM), the Relaxation Response (RR), the Center for Mind-Body Medicine's (CMBM) program, and hatha yoga programs. All of these practices have been used in educational settings, while in clinical, hospital, residential, juvenile justice, and home settings MBIs (including mindfulness-based stress reduction:MBSR, mindfulness-based cognitive therapy: MBCT, dialectical behavior therapy:DBT, and acceptance and commitment therapy:ACT) have proliferated.

The particular practice or intervention may be chosen to address unique challenges. In addition, the setting constraints may eliminate some practices. For example, Felver, Doerner, Jones, Kaye, and Merrell (2013) acknowledge the secular foundations of public school settings and the importance of maintaining a transparent approach when offering mindfulness programs in schools.

Some settings and circumstances may call for a standardized program while other situations call for a program uniquely tailored for a particular population. In schools, younger adolescents may benefit from universal social and emotional learning programs (with a mindfulness component) while older adolescents are more likely to be offered targeted mindfulness and meditation programs. Adolescents in clinical, hospital, residential, juvenile justice, and home settings may be offered a wide range of mindfulness-based interventions (MBIs) chosen to treat the particular challenges of the adolescents. For example, MBSR is used to treat a wide range of psychological and medical concerns, while MBCT helps to prevent relapse of major depression.

Dialectical Behavior Therapy is especially helpful for treating those diagnosed with Borderline Personality Disorder and comorbid non-suicidal self-jury, while ACT is used to help people struggling with pain. The RR and TM methods are well-suited for use in schools to help students decrease anxiety and increase self-regulation and attention while enhancing stress management. Alternatively, the CMBM's mind-body program is particularly well-suited for use in communities affected by traumatic events. However, some adolescents will be better served by providing a unique program, rather than a standardized approach. This is particularly the case when student ownership of the programming is crucial to the empowerment of students and to the success of the program (Wisner & Starzec, 2016).

In addition to the setting and the type of intervention used, program planning will include decisions about how to deliver the method and who will deliver the practice or program. These decisions have important implications for the success of the program.

Provider of Instruction and Delivery Method

Mindfulness and meditation practices and programs are traditionally delivered through individual or group face-to-face instruction. Teachers and facilitators have included primary and secondary school teachers, counselors and therapists, medical and psychiatric personnel, meditation teachers, and parents.

The teacher of the practice often depends upon the setting. For school-based programs, Sanger and Dorjee (2015) suggest that mindfulness training has relied too strongly on outside trainers and could be more sustained by promoting a personal practice for teachers and training teachers to deliver mindfulness programs. However, schools with limited funds and scarce resources may look to professionals in the surrounding communities (who are willing to donate time and resources) to implement mindfulness and meditation programs (Wisner & Starzec, 2016).

Trained counselors and therapists, employed by an institution, are likely to deliver programs and teach mindfulness and meditation practices in clinical, hospital, and residential settings. However, there are times, particularly in juvenile justice settings and correctional settings, when a meditation teacher not employed by the institution will provide the instruction. In home settings, parents typically serve as the primary meditation teachers.

New methods of delivering and teaching practices and programs, discussed later in this chapter, include audio-guided programs, apps for mobile phones, and computer options. There is limited information about these options in the literature, but given the prevalence of technology in contemporary societies, it is likely that these options will be used more frequently in the future. In addition to addressing provider of instruction and delivery method, dosage of the interventions must be selected.

Dosage of the Intervention and Home Practice

The dosage (i.e., the frequency and duration) of the mindfulness and meditation practice and the level of home practice are choices that are made prior to program provision (Moore, Gruber, Derose, & Malinowski, 2012; Quach, Gibler, & Mano, 2016). For example, programs adapted for adolescents (e.g., MBSR-T, MBCT-C, DBT-T, and ACT for teens) involve adaptations to the programs designed for adults. These adjustments may include briefer group session duration, adjustments in the frequency of sessions, adaptation of the language and discussion topics to reach adolescents, additional facilitators, briefer duration of experiential mindfulness or meditation practices, variations in home practice, and elimination of a day-long retreat component (for MBSR) (Biegel, Brown, Shapiro, & Schubert, 2009; Greco, Blomquist, Acra, & Moulton, 2008; Rathus & Miller, 2014; Sanger & Dorjee, 2015; Semple, Lee, Rosa, & Miller, 2010). Thus, the literature offers helpful guidance for adapting programs to meet the needs of adolescents.

Home practice is typically an important component of mindfulness-based programs and decisions must be made about recommendations for the frequency and length of home practice. Supportive aspects of home practice include methods to monitor practice and use of audio or video resources to encourage home practice (Deplus et al., 2016; Sibinga et al., 2011; Singh et al., 2011).

Teaching Mindfulness and Meditation to Adolescents

Teaching face-to-face individual and group mindfulness and meditation practices involves preparation and necessitates particular skills (Crane et al., 2010, 2012). As such, there are personal qualities and professional qualifications necessary for teaching these practices to adolescents. These qualities and qualifications prepare instructors to provide effective services to program participants and allow them to prepare for challenges that may occur during program delivery. Developing the qualities and qualifications is a process, and integrity must ultimately guide the teaching of these practices to youth (Saltzman, 2014).

Qualities and Qualifications for Teachers, Facilitators, and Clinicians

Perhaps the most important factor for successful teaching of mindfulness and meditation practices is the establishment of a personal practice. This supports the other qualities helpful for teaching mindfulness and meditation and provides a foundation for professional development. This also is true for clinicians who wish to use these practices in their work.

Personal Mindfulness or Meditation Practice

A daily mindfulness or meditation practice, over an extended time period, is recommended for those who wish to incorporate these practices into their work. Establishment of a personal mindfulness or meditation practice may occur in a number of ways. Many people learn meditation through a spiritual or religious program (e.g., Buddhist meditation programs, Christian meditation programs, indigenous teachings, hatha yoga programs). Others learn mindfulness skills and meditation practices in the course of secular continuing education and training programs (e.g., the Center for Mindfulness in Medicine, Health Care, and Society, the Center for Mind-Body Medicine, the Benson-Henry Institute, the Centre for Mindfulness Research and Practice). These options are discussed later in this chapter and a comprehensive, but not exhaustive, list of secular resources is offered at the end of the chapter.

Personal Qualities

With daily mindfulness and meditation practice over an extended period of time, personal qualities such as honesty, respect, compassion, empathy, acceptance, and a non-judgmental attitude are fostered (Saltzman, 2014). Another personal quality that emerges with sustained practice is an aura of authenticity (Woods, 2009). The ability to model and personify these qualities as cultivated through a mindfulness or meditation practice also are developed (Crane et al., 2010, 2012). In addition, a sense of openness and awareness of bodily sensations and movements occurs in the absence of a need to control or change experiences (Woods, 2009).

Professional Qualifications

Working with adolescents can be rewarding and invigorating. There are challenges as well, but those who work with adolescents are committed to empowering them despite these challenges. Daily mindfulness or meditation practice and cultivation of personal qualities supports this professional dedication to helping adolescents. A number of other factors support those who wish to incorporate mindfulness and meditation into their work with adolescents.

For example, knowledge of adolescent development and familiarity with theories related to adolescence (e.g., developmental neuroscience, positive youth development, cognitive-behavioral theory, the systems and ecological perspectives, identity development, and the transtheoretical model of change) are necessary elements for those providing services to adolescents. This knowledge, with a commitment to using a strengths-based approach, provides a foundation for working with adolescents in educational, community, or clinical settings.

Teaching mindfulness and meditation group-based programming, including MBSR and MBCT, necessitates particular training and skills. For example, preparation is needed to foster competent teaching of the content of the practice, a solid understanding of group process is necessary, and an ability to help participants process their experiences is required (Crane et al., 2010, 2012; Woods, 2009). Teachers and facilitators must be able to forge a connection with participants while creating and maintaining a sense of safety for participants (Saltzman, 2014). In addition, maintaining personal boundaries in a mindful manner supports wellness for the teacher and security for the participant (Rechtschaffen, 2014). In addition, mindfulness and meditation practices may bring about uncomfortable responses for youth with unresolved emotions due to trauma. Thus, a meditation teacher or facilitator needs to be educated about the role of stress and trauma in relation to practices such as mindfulness, meditation, and yoga (Rechtschaffen, 2014). A helpful discussion of these topics is offered by Payne, Levine, and Crane-Godreau (2015). Some programs are specifically designed to help those who have experienced trauma. For example, the CMBM's program is specifically designed to work with those who have been exposed to traumatic events. The program uses innovative methods to address these concerns (e.g., meditation and movement activities, guided imagery, autogenic training, simple biofeedback exercises, creative writing, and drawing exercises) (Staples, Abdel Atti, & Gordon, 2011).

Experience teaching movement practices, such as yoga, qigong, or Tai Chi Chuan, is helpful for mindfulness, MBSR, and MBCT teachers and facilitators (Woods, 2009). In addition, access to supervision by an experienced meditation teacher is helpful (Crane et al., 2010, 2012).

There are efforts to evaluate teachers on the skills necessary for successful delivery of programming. For example, The Manual of Mindfulness-based

Interventions Teaching Assessment Criteria prepared by the Universities of Bangor, Exeter, and Oxford offers a method for evaluating teaching qualities through six domains. Teachers are assessed on how materials are presented and organized in sessions, skills in connecting with participants, personification of mindfulness, how they lead mindfulness practices, teaching and discussion skills, and the maintenance of group process (https://www.bangor.ac.uk/mindfulness/documents/MBI-TACmanualsummaryaddendums05-16.pdf). This approach not only helps teachers gauge skills necessary for program delivery, but could be useful in program evaluation.

Engagement in professional training programs provides opportunities for learning about the background of mindfulness and meditation programs and offers opportunities to practice the skills needed to successfully facilitate these programs. In addition, regular participation in mindfulness or meditation retreats is recommended as this supports the facilitator's own personal mindfulness and meditation practice (Woods, 2009).

Postgraduate Programs and Professional Development

Postgraduate programs and professional trainings for those wishing to incorporate mindfulness, including MBSR and MBCT, into their clinical work are available through a number of universities and organizations. A master's degree in mindfulness is offered through the Centre for Mindfulness Research and Practice at Bangor University in North Wales. Students learn general mindfulness skills and the curriculum for MBSR and MBCT. The Centre also offers the MBSR and MBCT courses and a postgraduate diploma in teaching mindfulness-based courses, as well as continuing education for professionals wishing to integrate mindfulness approaches in their clinical work.

Professional training in MBSR also is available through organizations such as the Center for Mindfulness in Medicine, Health Care, and Society, Duke Integrative Medicine, University of California at San Diego Center for Mindfulness, the Institute for Mindfulness-Based Approaches, The Centre for Mindfulness Studies in Toronto, and the Centre for Mindfulness Ireland. Professional training in MBCT also is available through organizations such as the Oxford Mindfulness Centre, The Centre for Mindfulness Studies in Toronto, and the University of California at San Diego Center for Mindfulness, and the Institute for Mindfulness-Based Approaches in Europe. In addition, MBSR-T training is offered through the organization Stressed Teens.

Professional trainings in diverse school-based mindfulness programs also are available. Information about these trainings are available through organizations such as the Hawn Foundation, the Learning to BREATHE program, the Mindfulness in Schools Project's .b program, and the Mindful Schools program. Other organizations offering trainings including The Inner Kids Program and the Inner Resilience Program.

Professional training also is available for learning to facilitate the meditation programs discussed in this chapter. These include the CMBM group program (training and certification) and the Benson-Henry Institute for Mind Body Medicine's programming (including the RR). In addition, information about becoming certified to teach the TM technique is available from the Enlightened Leadership International organization. The prospective TM teacher first learns the TM method and fees are paid to the TM organization. The fee for TM pays for initial TM training plus follow-up sessions. Part of the tuition is used for scholarships to support programs for school children, veterans with post-traumatic stress disorder, homeless adults and children, and American Indians on reservations (Rosenthal, 2012).

Challenges in Teaching Mindfulness to Adolescents

Teaching and facilitating mindfulness and meditation programs for adolescents is typically a rewarding experience. Guiding youth in these practices and seeing them develop self-awareness and self-regulation skills is gratifying. Watching them become happier and more engaged with others is satisfying. Even so, personal, programmatic, and ecological challenges may arise in the process.

Emotional, cognitive, and behavioral challenges may be encountered, especially early in the process of learning mindfulness and meditation skills. Some adolescents experience uncomfortable feelings during meditation. These include boredom, sadness, mistrust, fear, feeling uncomfortable with silence, or sensations of re-experiencing trauma. Adolescents also may believe that meditation is not personally relevant, they may have negative preconceptions toward meditation, or may find meditation is not helpful to them. Adolescents may have difficulty concentrating and focusing during meditation and may experience distracting thoughts. Physical or emotional discomfort may occur during mindfulness or meditation practices (e.g., drowsiness, inactivity of seated practice, pain experienced during meditation practice, trying a practice with eyes closed, or prioritizing basic needs) (Barnert et al., 2014; Bögels, Hoogstad, van Dun, De Shutter, & Restifo, 2008; Grabbe, Nguy, & Higgins, 2012; Wisner & Starzec, 2016).

Other barriers to effective programming are faced when adolescents are reluctant to participate in practices or programs, do not complete assigned tasks or programs due to disinterest, or are discharged from a placement before completing the program. Challenges in programming also may be encountered when the physical setting is inhospitable to mindfulness and meditation exercises (Bögels et al., 2008; Semple et al., 2010; Wisner & Starzec, 2016).

Careful program planning, and a teacher or facilitator who possesses the qualities discussed earlier in this chapter, can minimize or eliminate many of these challenges. For the teacher, forming effective working relationships with participants allows exploration of these concerns often with satisfying results. Effective coaching, within a trusting relationship, can assist participants in optimizing mindfulness and meditation practices. For example, using meditation techniques such as counting breaths and labeling thoughts can minimize cognitive barriers for some participants. Dynamic and interactive sessions may help to alleviate behavioral challenges and modification of program components may assist vulnerable adolescents. Knowledge of adolescent development can guide decisions and responses in the face of these challenges. In addition, normalizing psycho-social, cognitive, and behavioral challenges of learning mindfulness and meditation practices, many of which also occur for adults learning meditation, can minimize many of these barriers (Barnert, Himelstein, Herbert, Garcia-Romeu, & Chamberlain, 2014; Bögels et al., 2008; Grabbe et al., 2012; Wisner & Starzec, 2016).

Physical environment challenges may be overcome through brainstorming options for addressing barriers such as noise or room limitations. For example, incorporating audio meditations with soothing background sounds may be an option for overcoming noise barriers. Allowing youth to take a leadership role in decisions such as these also may minimize some challenges (Wisner & Starzec, 2016).

Future Directions for Mindfulness and Meditation for Adolescents

The literature about teaching mindfulness and meditation to adolescents has focused on providing instruction through face-to-face methods taught to individuals or groups. However, other delivery options are beginning to receive attention in the literature.

Program Delivery Options

Emerging literature offers information about new delivery options for teaching mindfulness and meditation practices including audio-guided programs, phone, and computer options. For example, a 10-minute audio-guided mindful-based social-emotional learning awareness training program based on MBSR was offered to 191 students in two US public elementary schools (Bakosh, Snow, Tobias, Houlihan, & Barbosa-Leiker, 2016). The 8-week school-based program involved using daily practice to progress through 35 different audio mindfulness exercises. Compared to a control group, those in the mindfulness-based program showed enhanced quarterly reading grades and improvements in classroom behavior. The authors pointed out that the program is flexible because it does not require an expert mindfulness teacher and does not depend on teacher knowledge to deliver the program. Teachers participated in the program in the classroom alongside students with no curriculum changes or special classroom changes.

In another study, a cell phone app used to deliver a mindfulness program for adolescents showed promise for managing stress in 16 US adolescents of diverse ethnic backgrounds (Donovan et al., 2016). Daily use of the app ranged from 6–26 days (mean of 16.8 days) over the course of the 30-day program. A majority of the participants enjoyed using the app and found it easy to navigate and understand. Themes from focus group data indicated that the app was soothing and relaxing and brought about feelings of happiness and gratitude. Participants reported benefits related to an ability to focus on feelings and learning relaxation skills. Suggestions for improvement included increasing personalization and being able to share the experiences with others (Donovan et al., 2016).

Tunney, Cooney, Coyle, and O'Reilly (2016) compared the experience of learning mindfulness through computer-based avatar technology with a program offered in a face-to-face delivery method. Participants, from a nonclinical population, were 93 Irish children between 10 and 12 years of age. One group of students watched a computer program with an avatar leading mindfulness exercises. The other group of students were taught mindfulness through guided meditation exercises facilitated by one of the authors of the study. Analysis of qualitative data showed that both groups reported being engaged in the program while experiencing enhanced attention, relaxation, awareness, and letting go of thoughts (Tunney et al., 2016). Qualitative data showed that face-to-face participants reported active cognitive experiences and the sense of being soothed; but, they also mentioned feeling tired during the mindfulness exercises. On the other hand, those using the computerized mindfulness exercises reported a sense of peacefulness and the ability to engage in meta-cognition. Thus, while there were many similarities between the two groups, there also were some differences that merit additional investigation.

While these are innovative interventions for nonclinical populations, it is likely that these simplified versions of mindfulness and meditation program delivery options, in the absence of personal coaching, would have limited usefulness for clinical populations. Group discussion and personal guidance by a mindfulness or meditation teacher are important aspects of programming for mindfulness and meditation interventions. These components of programming are particularly important for youth struggling with emotional or physical challenges.

Global and Cultural Considerations

Mindfulness and meditation programs are being used in diverse settings across the globe. However, there is limited discussion of cultural considerations for teaching mindfulness and meditation and for creation of culturally sensitive programs. Teaching mindfulness necessitates an inclusive approach that recognizes and respects diverse identities of race, gender, and sexual orientation. This can be managed through acknowledging historical factors, a constructivist approach, and recognizing the importance of lived experiences for those practicing mindfulness and meditation (McCown, 2015).

An example of how these cultural considerations may be used in an acceptance and mindfulness approach is provided by Hinton, Pich, Hofmann, and Otto (2013). They discuss Culturally Adapted CBT (CA-CBT) for Southeast Asian refugees and Latino populations. The goal of this approach is to increase psychological flexibility and emotion regulation while decreasing physiological distress, rumination, and attentional bias to threat.

In addition, research support for the potential of an MBI to reduce stress among incarcerated ethnic minority youth is offered by Le and Proulx (2015). This program was well-received by mixed-ethnic Native Hawaiian/Pacific Islander youths and offers an example of incorporation of cultural factors in mindfulness and meditation programs. The program used culturally sensitive components and included a facilitator who was a cultural leader in the community. The facilitator was able to provide connections between mindfulness practices and cultural beliefs. In other research supporting cultural factors in programming, Toomey and Anhalt (2016) suggest that mindfulness strategies may be a helpful coping strategy for sexual minority youth exposed to victimization.

The proliferation of the CMBMs programs illustrate the organization's commitment to serving people around the globe. The mind-body programs help people heal after traumatic experiences while fostering social justice and cultural empowerment. These programs are offered with an understanding of historical factors that have contributed to poverty, oppression, and marginalization in communities. The CMBMs website offers examples of how these programs are being implemented in such locations as Gaza, Israel, Haiti, Kosovo, and the Pine Ridge and Rosebud Reservations in South Dakota (https://cmbm.org). These programs offer uplifting examples of providing culturally sensitive programming to diverse cultural groups in locations across the globe. The programs provide rich examples for those offering mindfulness and meditation practices and programs for youth and for those conducting research on these topics.

Research Considerations

Much of the research on mindfulness and meditation programs for adolescents is preliminary and exploratory in nature. However, there are some controlled studies and several systematic reviews and meta-analyses show that mindfulness and meditation practices and programs have many benefits for adolescents (Black, 2015; Felver, Celis-de Hoyos, Tezanos, & Singh, 2016; Zenner, Herrnleben-Kurz, & Walach, 2014; Zoogman, Goldberg, Hoyt, & Miller, 2015). Black's (2015) review of mindfulness training for children and adolescents found a number of benefits. These included improvements in prosocial skills, self-regulation, and attention. Participants in mindfulness training also experienced reductions in anxiety, depression, perceived stress, blood pressure, and heart rate. Zoogman et al. (2015), in their meta-analytic study of mindfulness interventions for children and adolescents, suggested that these practices are particularly helpful for reducing anxiety and depression in clinical populations.

Furthermore, in a meta-analytic study of school-based mindfulness programs for children and adolescents, Zenner, Herrnleben-Kurz, and Walach (2014), found that these programs improved cognitive performance, enhanced resiliency, and reduced stress. In addition, Felver et al. (2016) conducted a systematic review of MBIs for youth in school settings. They found that MBIs increased levels of mindfulness and lead to improvements in physiological functioning, positive affect, optimism, coping, emotion regulation, social-emotional competence, social skills, classroom engagement, and classroom behavior. In addition, decreased behavioral problems, anxiety, depression, affective disturbances, executive functioning problems, and suicidal ideation were noted for children and adolescents who participated in MBIs (Felver et al., 2016).

These reviews and meta-analytic studies show that there are a wide range of biological, psychological, and social benefits of mindfulness-based programs for adolescents. While there are individual studies establishing cultural benefits of participation in mindfulness and meditation programs (Derezotes, 2000; Foret et al., 2012; Grabbe, Nguy, & Higgins, 2012; Wall, 2005), these cultural benefits were not mentioned in the review and meta-analytic studies. It is likely that the emphasis on secular practice with adolescents contributed to this, and that measuring potential outcomes related to cultural factors will occur in future research.

More research is needed, and additional controlled studies and new meta-analyses will emerge. In particular, meta-analyses of studies on meditation programs for adolescents (e.g., studies of TM and RR) would significantly contribute to the existing literature. Future research will foster a more complete understanding of what mindfulness and meditation practices for adolescents have to offer. For example, Felver et al. (2013) suggest that more information is needed to clarify the relationship between the role of attention and the benefits of mindfulness interventions. In addition, Felver et al. (2016) make a number of recommendations for school-based research. However, these recommendations also have relevance for future research in other settings as well. The authors recommended use of experimental design with random assignment and active comparison conditions in future research. They also call for additional meta-analytic studies and suggest that research replicate intervention effects of current MBIs and make an effort to explore analysis of treatment components. In addition, they recommend that participant characteristics and community information be described in detail and that collection and analysis of follow-up data be incorporated into studies. They suggest incorporation of multiple outcome measures. Felver et al. (2016) also suggest that a valid topic of future research is information about the level of training and experience needed to effectively deliver MBIs.

Moreover, Sanger and Dorjee (2015) suggest that program evaluations be tailored to study specific neurological and cognitive processes brought about by particular practices. In addition, differentiating between state and trait mindfulness may be useful for future research as well. Mindfulness and meditation may either lead to changes in states (e.g., changes in attentional abilities mediated by modifications in brain structure and function) or traits (e.g., protection from cognitive decline) (Chiesa & Serretti, 2010). In addition, the integration of self-report measures, neurological measurements, and behavioral assessments in future research is recommended (Quach, Gibler, & Mano, 2016). More research is needed to address optimal intervention frequency and length of intervention and home practices (Sanger, & Dorjee, 2015; Soler et al., 2014). In addition, additional research exploring delivery methods is warranted given the opportunities presented by innovative options for program delivery.

Another area being explored more closely is the measurement of mindfulness. There are a limited number of mindfulness scales, and these scales may not provide a comprehensive assessment of mindfulness (Bergomi, Tschacher, & Kupper, 2013). Most of the scales are designed for adults, but some scales are developed for children and adolescents. One such scale, the Child and Adolescent Mindfulness Measure shows promise for measuring mindfulness skills in children and adolescents (Greco, Baer, & Smith, 2011). The authors acknowledge that additional research is needed on this instrument, but recognize that the measurement of mindfulness in research studies is an important factor in supporting future research with youth.

Mindfulness and meditation research has been plagued by the lack of precise theories to guide the research and by failure to provide a sound theoretical base to support findings (Sedlmeier et al., 2012). Clarification of theoretical foundations of the mindfulness and meditation practices will support future research efforts (Hölzel, Lazar, Gard, Schuman-Olivier, Vago, & Ott, 2011). This will provide a stronger foundation for incorporating appropriate theoretical contexts when designing services to adolescents and when conducting research with adolescents.

Much of the research on mindfulness and meditation research with youth has been conducted with the intention of helping youth overcome some sort of problem or deficit. However, research placing mindfulness and meditation programming in the context of positive psychology and positive youth development is beginning to emerge (Mendelson, Greenberg, Dariotis, Gould, Rhoades, & Leaf, 2010; Waters, 2011).

This is an important area of investigation that will contribute to understanding how to help youth thrive as they move forward developmentally.

These are just a few examples of topics of interest to those conducting research on mindfulness and meditation practices and programs for adolescents. More issues of importance will emerge as the literature expands. Investigators who address these factors are better prepared to engage in successful research programs. Future research studies will contribute to the knowledge base about the benefits and long-term effects of mindfulness and meditation programs.

Summary

The evidence suggests that benefits of mindfulness and meditation for adolescents are wide-ranging and encompass the biological, psychological, social, and cultural realms of development. This research supports the importance of integrating theory, research, and practice to understand the potential outcomes when offering mindfulness and meditation programs for adolescents. The integration of mindfulness and meditation practices and programs with principles of cultural sensitivity and positive youth development offers exciting opportunities to foster adolescents in their personal journeys and developmental activities. The future is sure to bring additional innovative programs and practices and more rigorous research about the efficacy of these programs.

Those who plan to implement mindfulness and meditation programs are confronted with many decisions in the program development process. Decisions are made during this process including choice of appropriate interventions or practices that best fit the needs of the program participants, types of delivery methods, and choice of facilitator. The current literature offers guidance for making these programming decisions, and future research will provide additional information.

Teaching mindfulness and meditation to adolescents is a rewarding activity for those working with youth. There are many options available for obtaining training and pursuing educational opportunities for those interested in this course of action. These opportunities are available across many geographical locations and provide options for implementing mindfulness and meditation into personal and professional lives. Some of these resources for professional development and postgraduate educational opportunities are listed at the end of this chapter.

Resources

Professional Development and Postgraduate Education

Organization/Institution	*Website*
Center for Mind-Body Medicine	https://cmbm.org
Center for Mindfulness in Medicine, Healthcare, and Society	http://www.umassmed.edu/cfm/
Center for Mindfulness at the University of California at San Diego	https://health.ucsd.edu/specialties/mindfulness/Pages/default.aspx
The Centre for Mindfulness Ireland	http://cfmi.ie
The Centre for Mindfulness Studies	http://www.mindfulnessstudies.com
Centre for Mindfulness Research and Practice	https://www.bangor.ac.uk/mindfulness/
Duke Integrative Medicine	https://www.dukeintegrativemedicine.org/programs-training/professionals/mindfulness-training-for-professionals/
Enlightened Leadership International	http://www.enlightenedleadershipprogram.org/tm-teacher-training
The Inner Kids Program	http://www.susankaisergreenland.com/inner-kids-program.html
The Inner Resilience Program	http://www.innerresilience.com/index.html
The Institute for Mindfulness-Based Approaches	http://www.institute-for-mindfulness.org
Learning to BREATHE	http://learning2breathe.org
Mindful Schools Program	http://www.mindfulschools.org
The Mindfulness in Schools Project (.b)	https://mindfulnessinschools.org/courses/dotb/
MindUP	http://thehawnfoundation.org
Oxford Mindfulness Centre	http://www.oxfordmindfulness.org
The Resilient Schools Program	The Resilient Schools Program (The Benson-Henry Institute)
Stressed Teens (MBSR-T)	http://www.stressedteens.com

References

Bakosh, L. S., Snow, R. M., Tobias, J. M., Houlihan, J. L., & Barbosa-Leiker, C. (2016). Maximizing mindful learning: An innovative mindful awareness intervention improves elementary school students' quarterly grades. *Mindfulness, 7*(1), 59–67.

Barnert, E. S., Himelstein, S., Herbert, S., Garcia-Romeu, A., & Chamberlain, L. J. (2014). Exploring an intensive meditation intervention for incarcerated youth. *Child and Adolescent Mental Health, 19*(1), 69–73.

Bergomi, C., Tschacher, W., & Kupper, Z. (2013). The assessment of mindfulness with self-report measures: Existing scales and open issues. *Mindfulness*, *4*(3), 191–202.

Biegel, G. M, Brown, K. W., Shapiro, S. L, & Schubert, C. (2009). Mindfulness-based stress reduction for the treatment of adolescent psychiatric outpatients: A randomized clinical trial. *Journal of Clinical and Consulting Psychology*, *77*(5), 855–866.

Black, D. S. (2015). Mindfulness training for children and adolescents: A state-of-the-science review. In K. W. Brown, R. M. Ryan, & J. D. Creswell (Eds.), Handbook of mindfulness: Theory and research (pp. 283–310). New York, NY: Guilford Press.

Bögels, S., Hoogstad, B., Van Dun, L., De Shutter, S., & Restifo, K. (2008). Mindfulness training for adolescents with externalising disorders and their parents. *Behavioural and Cognitive Psychotherapy*, *36*, 193–209.

Chiesa, A., & Serretti, A. (2010). A systematic review of neurobiological and clinical features of mindfulness meditations. *Psychological Medicine*, *40*(08), 1239–1252.

Crane, R. S., Kuyken, W., Hastings, R., Rothwell, N., & Williams, J. M. G. (2010). Training teachers to deliver mindfulness-based interventions: learning from the UK experience. *Mindfulness*, *1*(2), 74–86. doi:10.1007/s12671-010-0010-9.

Crane R.S., Kuyken, W., Williams, J. M. G., Hastings, R., Cooper, L., & Fennell, M.J.V. (2012), Competence in teaching mindfulness-based courses: Concepts, development, and assessment. *Mindfulness*, *3*(1), 76–84. DOI: 10.1007/s12671-011-0073-2.

Deplus, S., Billieux, J., Scharff, C., & Philippot, P. (2016). A mindfulness-based group intervention for enhancing self-regulation of emotion in late childhood and adolescence: A pilot study. *International Journal of Mental Health and Addiction*, *14*(5), 775–790.

Derezotes, D. (2000). Evaluation of yoga and meditation trainings with adolescent sex offenders. *Child and Adolescent Social Work Journal*, *17*(2), 97–113.

Donovan, E., Rodgers, R. F., Cousineau, T. M., McGowan, K. M., Luk, S., Yates, K., & Franko, D. L. (2016). Brief report: Feasibility of a mindfulness and self-compassion based mobile intervention for adolescents. *Journal of Adolescence*, *53*, 217–221.

Felver, J. C., Celis-De Hoyos, C. E., Tezanos, K., & Singh, N. N. (2016). A systematic review of mindfulness-based interventions for youth in school settings. *Mindfulness*, *7*(1), 34–45.

Felver, J. C., Doerner, E., Jones, J., Kaye, N. C., & Merrell, K. W. (2013). Mindfulness in school psychology: Applications for intervention and professional practice. *Psychology in the Schools*, *50*(6), 531–547. DOI:10.1002/pits.21695

Foret, M. M., Scult, M., Wilcher, M., Chudnofsky, R., Malloy, L., Hasheminejad, N., & Park, E. R. (2012). Integrating a relaxation response-based curriculum into a public high school in Massachusetts. *Journal of Adolescence*, *35*(2), 325–332.

Grabbe, L., Nguy, S. T., & Higgins, M. K. (2012). Spirituality development for homeless youth: A mindfulness meditation feasibility pilot. *Journal of Child and Family Studies*, *21*(6), 925–937.

Greco, L. A., Baer, R. A., & Smith, G. T. (2011). Assessing mindful-ness in children and adolescents: Development and validation of the Child and Adolescent Mindfulness Measure (CAMM). *Psychological Assessment*, *23*, 606–614.

Greco, L. A., Blomquist, K. K., Acra, S., & Moulton, D. (2008). Acceptance and commitment therapy for adolescents with functional abdominal pain: Results of a pilot investigation. *Unpublished Manuscript*.

Himelstein, S., Hastings, A., Shapiro, S., & Heery, M. (2012). Mindfulness training for self-regulation and stress with incarcerated youth A pilot study. *Probation Journal*, *59*(2), 151–165.

Hinton, D. E., Pich, V., Hofmann, S. G., & Otto, M. W. (2013). Acceptance and mindfulness techniques as applied to refugee and ethnic minority populations with PTSD: Examples from "Culturally Adapted CBT." *Cognitive and Behavioral Practice*, *20*(1), 33–46.

Hölzel, B. K., Lazar, S. W., Gard, T., Schuman-Olivier, Z., Vago, D. R., & Ott, U. (2011). How does mindfulness meditation work? Proposing mechanisms of action from a conceptual and neural perspective. *Perspectives on psychological science*, *6*(6), 537–559.

Le, T. N., & Proulx, J. (2015). Feasibility of mindfulness-based intervention for incarcerated mixed-ethnic Native Hawaiian/Pacific Islander youth. *Asian American Journal of Psychology*, *6*(2), 181.

McCown, D. (2015). *Teaching mindfulness with mindfulness of diversity in Resources for Teaching Mindfulness: An International Handbook*. Retrieved from https://www.mindandlife.org/wp-content/uploads/2016/01/Magee-Teaching-Mindfulness-With-Mindfulness-of-Diversity.pdf

Meiklejohn, J., Phillips, C. & Freedman, M. L., Griffin, M. L., Biegel, G. & Roach, A., Frank, J... Saltzman, A. (2012). Integrating mindfulness training into K-12 education: Fostering the resilience of teachers and students. *Mindfulness*, *1*(1), 1–17.

Mendelson, T., Greenberg, M. T., Dariotis, J. K., Gould, L. F., Rhoades, B. L., & Leaf, P. J. (2010). Feasibility and preliminary outcomes of a school-based mindfulness intervention for urban youth. *Journal of Abnormal Child Psychology*, *38*(7), 985–994.

Moore, A., Gruber, T., Derose, J., & Malinowski, P. (2012). Regular, brief mindfulness meditation practice improves electrophysiological markers of attentional control. *Frontiers in Human Neuroscience*, 6, 18. http://doi.org/10.3389/fnhum.2012.00018

Nash, J. D. & Newberg, A. B. (2013). *Toward a unifying taxonomy and definition for meditation*. Jefferson Myrna Brind Center of Integration Medicine Faculty Papers. Paper 11. http://jdc.jefferson.edu/jmbcimfp/11

Payne, P., Levine, P. A., & Crane-Godreau, M. A. (2015). Somatic experiencing: using interoception and proprioception as core elements of trauma therapy. *Frontiers in Psychology, 6*(93). doi: 10.3389/fpsyg.2015.00093

Quach, D., Gibler, R. C., & Mano, K. E. J. (2016). Does home practice compliance make a difference in the effectiveness of mindfulness interventions for adolescents? *Mindfulness, 8*(2), 495–504.

Rathus, J. H., & Miller, A. L. (2014). *DBT® Skills Manual for Adolescents*. New York, NY: Guilford Publications.

Rechtschaffen, D. (2014). *The way of mindful education: Cultivating well-being in teachers and students*. New York, NY: WW Norton & Company.

Rosenthal, N. E. (2012). *Transcendence: Healing and Transformation through Transcendental Meditation*. New York, NY: Tarcher/Penguin.

Sanger, K. L., & Dorjee, D. (2015). Mindfulness training for adolescents: A neurodevelopmental perspective on investigating modifications in attention and emotion regulation using event-related brain potentials. *Cognitive, Affective, & Behavioral Neuroscience, 15*(3), 696–711.

Saltzman, A. (2014). *A Still Quiet Place: A mindfulness program for teaching children and adolescents to ease stress and difficult emotions*. Oakland, CA: New Harbinger Publications.

Sedlmeier, P., Eberth, J., Schwarz, M., Zimmermann, D., Haarig, F., Jaeger, S., & Kunze, S. (2012). The psychological effects of meditation: A meta-analysis. *Psychological Bulletin, 138*(6), 1139–1171.

Semple, R. J., Lee, J., Rosa, D., & Miller, L. F. (2010). A randomized trial of mindfulness-based cognitive therapy for children: Promoting mindful attention to enhance social-emotional resiliency in children. *Journal of Child and Family Studies, 19*(2), 218–229.

Sibinga, E. M., Kerrigan, D., Stewart, M., Johnson, K., Magyari, T., & Ellen, J. M. (2011). Mindfulness-based stress reduction for urban youth. *The Journal of Alternative and Complementary Medicine, 17*(3), 213–218.

Singh, N. N., Lancioni, G. E., Manikam, R., Winton, A. S. W., Singh, A. N. A., Singh, J.,... Singh, A. D. A. (2011). A mindfulness-based strategy for self-management of aggressive behavior in adolescents with autism. *Research in Autism Spectrum Disorders, 5*, 1153–1158. DOI:10.1016/j.rasd.2010.12.012

Soler, J., Cebolla, A., Feliu-Soler, A., Demarzo, M. M., Pascual, J. C., Baños, R., & García-Campayo, J. (2014). Relationship between meditative practice and self-reported mindfulness: the MINDSENS composite index. *PloSone, 9*(1), e86622.

Staples, J. K., Abdel Atti, J. A., & Gordon, J. S. (2011). Mind-body skills groups for posttraumatic stress disorder and depression symptoms in Palestinian children and adolescents in Gaza. *International Journal of Stress Management, 18* (3), 246–262.

Toomey, R. B., & Anhalt, K. (2016). Mindfulness as a coping strategy for bias-based school victimization among Latina/o sexual minority youth. *Psychology of Sexual Orientation and Gender Diversity, 3*(4), 432–441.

Tunney, C., Cooney, P., Coyle, D., & O'Reilly, G. (2016). Comparing young people's experience of technology-delivered v. face-to-face mindfulness and relaxation: two-armed qualitative focus group study. *The British Journal of Psychiatry*. DOI:10.1192/bjp.bp.115.172783

Wall, R. B. (2005). Tai Chi and mindfulness based stress reduction in a Boston public middle school. *Journal of Pediatric Health Care, 19*(4), 230–237.

Waters, L. (2011). A review of school-based positive psychology interventions. *The Australian Educational and Developmental Psychologist, 28*(02), 75–90.

Wisner, B. L. (2013). Less stress, less drama, and experiencing monkey mind: Benefits and challenges of a school-based meditation program for adolescents. *School Social Work Journal, 38*(1), 49–63.

Wisner, B. L., & Starzec, J. J. (2016). The process of personal transformation for adolescents practicing mindfulness skills in an alternative school setting. *Child and Adolescent Social Work Journal, 33*(3), 245–257.

Woods, S. L. (2009). Training professionals in mindfulness: The heart of teaching. In F. Didonna (Ed.). *Clinical handbook of mindfulness* (pp. 463–475). New York, NY: Springer.

Zenner, C., Herrnleben-Kurz, S., & Walach, H. (2014). Mindfulness-based interventions in schools–a systematic review and metaanalysis. *Frontiers in Psychology, 5*, 603. http://doi.org/10.3389/fpsyg.2014.00603

Zoogman, S., Goldberg, S. B., Hoyt, W. T., & Miller, L. (2015). Mindfulness interventions with youth: A meta-analysis. *Mindfulness, 6*(2), 290–302.

Index

B.L. Wisner, *Mindfulness and Meditation for Adolescents*,
DOI 10.1057/978-1-349-95207-6

L

M